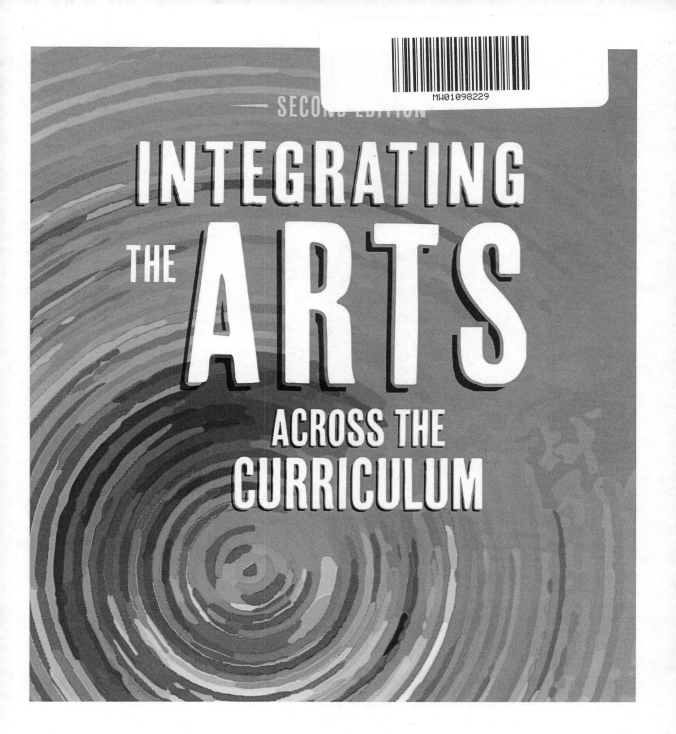

SECOND EDITION

INTEGRATING THE ARTS ACROSS THE CURRICULUM

Lisa Donovan, Ph.D.
Louise Pascale, Ph.D.

Publishing Credits

Corinne Burton, M.A.Ed., *Publisher*
Aubrie Nielsen, M.S.Ed., *EVP of Content Development*
Véronique Bos, *Creative Director*
Cathy Hernandez, *Senior Content Manager*
Laureen Gleason, *Editor*
David Slayton, *Assistant Editor*

Image Credits: Image Credits: p.34 Courtesy of E. Shea, Newburyport, Massachusetts.; p.42 Courtesy of Craig Norton; p.80 Courtesy of Heidi Hopwood, Idaho; p.105 Courtesy of E. Shea, Newburyport, Massachuetts; p.106 Courtesy of Hillary DesMarais; p.112 Courtesy of C. DeFilipp, Maine; p.125 Courtesy of Dana Schildkraut; p.127, 133 Courtesy of S. Fisher, Adjunct Faculty, Lesley University; p.128 Courtesy of Alex Edgerly (www.alexedgerly.com); p.131 Courtesy of Neel Badlani; p.152 Courtesy of Jacob's Pillow Curriculum in Motion; all other images from iStock Photo, Shutterstock and/or Envato Elements

A division of Teacher Created Materials

5482 Argosy Avenue
Huntington Beach, CA 92649-1039

www.tcmpub.com/shell-education

ISBN 978-0-7439-7036-5

© 2022 Shell Educational Publishing, Inc.

Printed by: **51307**
Printed In: **USA**
PO#: **11659**

Table of Contents

Foreword

In education, we're always tasked with "better." Better teaching practices, better test scores, better behaviors. This constant striving for improvement can lead to innovation. It can also lead to burnout.

As a former K-5 music educator, curriculum specialist, arts integration specialist, and founder of the Institute for Arts Integration and STEAM, I've seen my share of improvement measures in the last two decades. Some of them have made us better teachers and humans. Universal Design for Learning (UDL), cultural responsiveness, and social-emotional learning help us create meaningful and relevant learning experiences for all of our students. Yet many of these improvements have made our profession more challenging. An inordinate amount of focus on summative test scores and pre-scripted curriculum, and a move away from teacher-created resources and towards privately funded initiatives have left many educators struggling to teach with autonomy and differentiation to meet the rapidly changing needs of their students.

But there is hope for a better future. The arts integration approach has been a part of the fabric of education for decades. And the more research conducted and practical experiences shared, the more we're seeing the positive effects of integrating the arts in and through the standard curriculum model. It's clear that arts integration positively impacts student learning, student behaviors, social-emotional needs, and teacher efficacy. Still, the approach is laced with misconceptions and concerns: lack of time, lack of dedicated arts educators, and becoming "one more thing" to add to teachers' overflowing plates.

This is why Lisa Donovan and Louise Pascale's book is a critical read for 21st century educators. It offers a non-threatening, practical application for any and every educator to use arts integration strategies and methodology. Reading this book makes you feel like you can use any of the strategies presented—even if you don't consider yourself an "artist." Donovan and Pascale begin with examining the practice of integration and highlighting how to truly embed it as a natural part of the curriculum process. They highlight the links between arts for art's sake, arts enhancement, and arts integration—and explain why each is an important part of a child's learning experience. And they acknowledge the difficulties in today's school environment, while supporting educators who are stressed and strained by the current testing focus through arts-integrated techniques that serve as an avenue for student achievement in all forms.

Perhaps what is most exciting in this latest edition is the intentional focus on addressing cultural responsiveness, UDL, social-emotional learning, and 21st century skills through the lens of arts integration. The way Donovan and Pascale weave these approaches together is critical for educators who are tasked with teaching all the children in their care. Through strategy and lesson samples from diverse artists, genres, and voices from the classroom, this book extends equity through example in a practical and relevant way that has been previously lacking in the field.

The book is dedicated to offering examples of arts-integrated strategies and lessons from six arts areas: poetry, music, storytelling, drama, visual arts, and creative movement. The inclusion of such a variety of art forms lends accessibility, and opens doors for educators who may not be comfortable in one area of the arts to try a different avenue. As someone who has taught arts integration strategies for over a decade, I am delighted with some of the fresh ideas presented in this text. Additionally, the authors invite the readers to view the text (and the accompanying series of strategy books) less as a linear method to be read from cover to cover, and more as an artistic process in itself. This is meant to be a palette that you dip into, mix, and paint into your unique lesson design.

Unlike some teaching texts that merely present the approach itself, Donovan and Pascale also take care to address specific challenges to the implementation of arts integration—including planning, assessment, and standards-alignment—and offer resources for educators to use in overcoming these challenges. Similarly, the book also provides real-world examples from educators who are successfully using the approach in their classrooms. This serves to move this text from theory to a practical resource that can be referenced many times throughout the year.

Arts integration has the ability to unlock the power of creativity in every child, every day. This book will help you make this a reality in your own classroom.

—Susan Riley
Founder and CEO
The Institute for Arts Integration and STEAM

Acknowledgments

We'd like to thank our colleagues for their contributions to this book. Their rich examples and insights have helped to shape this book.

Kerrie Bellisario

Dr. Berta Berriz

Dr. Jenn Bogard

Dr. Maureen Creegan-Quinquis

Susan J. Fisher

Susan Griss

Dr. Francine Jennings

Kristina Lamour Sansone

Dr. Margaret (Meg) Lippert

Celeste Miller

Dr. Mary Clare Powell

Sally Rogers

Dr. Prilly Sanville

Dana Schildkraut

Robert Shreefter

Dr. Kim Silbaugh

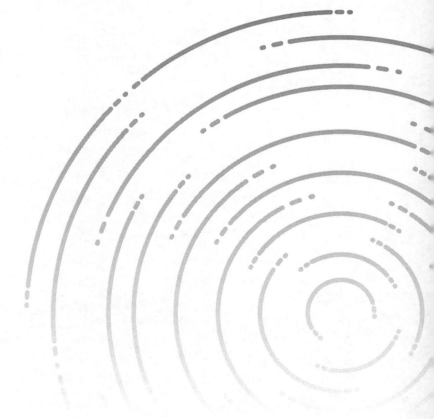

Preface

The first edition of this book, published in 2012, was generated by the enthusiasm and excitement teachers expressed having initiated arts integration into their curriculum. Educators often recognize and are eager to make changes so that learning is more accessible and more meaningful for every student. The challenge, however, is often not whether to make those changes but how to make them happen during an already filled-to-the-brim schedule. The discussion in this book explores how to make those changes happen.

This new edition is inspired by the many teachers with whom we have met and worked. Their voices and creative ideas are woven throughout this book. We envision the arts and arts integration becoming a mainstay of teaching and learning, thus stimulating innovation, curiosity, critical thinking, and new ways of being in the world (Diaz and McKenna 2017, 20).

Over the course of many years, after teaching about arts integration to teachers from across the country, we soon began to recognize the power the arts have for transforming not only the way students learn but how teachers think about teaching. They enthusiastically reported that their students, even those previously considered most challenging, were more engaged and excited about learning than ever before.

The book begins with investigations of six art forms: storytelling, drama, poetry, music, visual arts, and creative movement. In these chapters, we present basic information about the specific elements of each art form and investigate assumptions and perceptions. Following that, there are specific examples and ideas for integrating the arts in the curriculum for grades K–12, as well as suggestions for how arts integration can reinforce culturally responsive teaching and social-emotional learning. The ideas in this book also can be successfully adapted for learning in virtual and hybrid environments. Throughout these chapters, *In the Classroom* sections feature the voices of teachers who have successfully integrated the arts into their classrooms. The final chapter shows you the nuts and bolts of creating a unit of study using arts integration and a discussion of assessment.

We are pleased to offer you this newly revised edition of *Integrating the Arts Across the Curriculum*. A lot has happened in education and in the world since the first edition of this book was published, and it is important to recognize those changes. You may be wondering what's different in this new edition. We've taken time to update the resources and highlights of diverse voices in the field. In this revised text, we have addressed the following:

- the role the arts can play in the social-emotional health of students
- the need for culturally responsive teaching approaches
- the links between arts integration and Universal Design for Learning (UDL)

In addition, we offer the following:

- fresh ideas for strategies and rich examples from the field
- a new lens on assessment, with assessment options that meet the needs of all students
- an updated set of references and recommended resources

We hope you are as excited and inspired by this new edition as we are!

Introduction

Arts Integration: The Ripple Effect

What happens when the arts are integrated into the curriculum? What effect, if any, does integrating the arts have on students, teachers, curriculum, learning, and the classroom and school community? How does arts integration support culturally responsive teaching, differentiation, Universal Design for Learning (UDL), and social and emotional learning? The intention of this book is to explore these questions and dive deeper into the theory and practice of what it means to truly and authentically integrate the arts.

Imagine a still pool of water. A pebble, when dropped into the middle, splashes quietly. Slowly the ripples emerge and travel outward in expanding circles. It becomes clear that the consequence of this seemingly simple initial event, the dropping of the stone, goes far beyond the place where it started. The impact is far reaching. There is not only a surface ripple effect but also a ripple effect that is felt far beneath the surface.

Teachers enrolled in the Master's of Education in Integrated Teaching through the Arts (ITA) program with Lesley University were assigned the task of creating a metaphor or simile that accurately demonstrated the power of arts integration. They were asked to demonstrate what happens when the arts are infused into the curriculum as a learning and assessment tool.

Having experienced the arts themselves and with their students over a period of two years, they were put into small groups and challenged to come up with creative solutions to demonstrate the power of the arts through metaphor. One group thought of the arts as transformative—like yeast in bread dough or the startling change of moving from a black-and-white photo to color. Another group imagined arts integration like tending to a garden or traveling to unknown places. The solutions were imaginative and meaningful, each one illustrating how the arts transform, nurture, change things at a deeper level, and allow for multiple perspectives and multiple voices to be heard and honored.

One group decided on the metaphor of the ripple effect. They demonstrated this by filling a small pool with water and then throwing about 20 corks in the middle of the pool. The corks bobbed around, seemingly without any particular direction or relationship to one another. We all quietly stood over the pool, watching the corks. They seem to float aimlessly in the water. Then, someone dropped one stone right in the middle of the pool. Everything immediately changed.

The stone, having broken the surface, almost instantly disrupted the quiet pool and the bobbing corks. As the ripples began to spread, one circle multiplied into another and then another (Shafak 2010).

We stood in awe as we watched the corks, which were no longer aimlessly floating about, but moving, connecting, creating patterns, and working in synchronization. What became quickly apparent was that the total effect of the dropped stone was not immediately evident. The consequences went much deeper than what we witnessed on the surface. As we continued to observe the ripples, the connections between the ripple effect and integrating the arts became more and more evident and more profound.

What Is Arts Integration?

"Arts integration is the investigation of curricular content through artistic explorations. In this process, the arts provide an avenue for rigorous investigation, representation, expression, and reflection of both curricular content and the art form itself."

—Gene Diaz, Lisa Donovan, and Louise Pascale (2006)

For many educators, although the idea of integrating the arts seems appealing, the challenge of having to be "comfortable" in every art form seems overwhelming. "I can't do it," is a familiar response. "I'm not an artist. I can't draw. And for heaven's sake, don't ask me to sing!"

Integrating the arts is not about creating professional artists. It is about deepening learning and reaching students of every ability, ethnicity, and linguistic background. It is about teaching students who learn in a variety of ways, not just through reading and writing.

A common misconception about arts integration is that if we integrate the arts, we risk eliminating the art and music specialists. Nothing is further from the truth. We need both! Arts educators focus on teaching the specific skills and elements of a particular art form. In the classroom, the arts are a vehicle for strengthening the core curriculum, deepening and assessing learning. When the arts are integrated, learning is experienced in a variety of ways, allowing each student to be successful in various content areas.

Prominent educational leaders over time, such as Jonathan Kozol, Deborah Meier, Nel Noddings, Linda Darling-Hammond, Maxine Greene, Ken Robinson, Elliott Eisner, and others, have expressed the need to reform our educational system and nurture students to become creators, meaning-makers, and empathizers (Pink 2005). It was John Dewey (1931) who remarked that the problem lies "in our lack of imagination in generating leading ideas. Because we are afraid of speculative ideas, we do, and do over and over again, an immense amount of specialized work in the region of facts. We forget such facts are only data . . . uncompleted meanings, and unless they are rounded out into complete ideas—a work which can only be done by . . . a free imagination of intellectual possibilities—they are as helpless as are all maimed things."

The arts provide an approach that addresses these concerns by engaging students in their learning, developing curriculum where curiosity is central and students tap into their creativity while developing the skills they need for the twenty-first century, including creativity, collaboration, critical thinking, and communication. The corks, whether you think of them as curriculum content, individual students, or the entire classroom, no longer bob around aimlessly and in isolation; they react, respond, and interact.

When students learn about cells or molecules by actually "becoming" molecules through a movement exercise to internalize and personalize the understanding; when they write persona poems about who they are, what they do, and how they think and feel as lungs or blood cells; or when they dramatize, through a tableau experience, the meaning of the word *metamorphosis*, deep learning occurs. It goes way beyond the "right answer." Learning sticks and is meaningful and relevant. Students are indeed gaining twenty-first-century skills—creativity, critical thinking, communication, and collaboration—that are essential for higher-order thinking.

As Silverstein and Layne note, "Arts integration provides multiple ways for students to make sense of what they learn (construct understanding) and makes their learning visible (demonstrate understanding). It goes beyond the initial step of helping students learn and recall information to challenging students to take the information and facts they have learned and do something with them to build deeper understanding" (2010).

The Arts Are Not an Extra

A second-grade teacher writes about the difficulty of finding space for the arts in her curriculum, although she knows it is an effective tool to enhance learning for her students. She says, "Our district is currently using a prescribed basal program utilizing specific stories. We have little freedom or time to work or think outside the mandated box. Our students, as well as ourselves, have less opportunity to create and use imagination beyond the curriculum that everyone hears at the same time and in the same way."

Her dilemma is one that many educators across the country are facing. However, if we truly want children to learn, we must expand our strategies for teaching and learning in ways that reach the diverse learners who make up today's classrooms. It is not about "fitting" the arts into the curriculum but weaving them into the curriculum as a natural part of how the content is presented and assessed. The arts must be thought of as a foundation, the supporting structure that carries the importance of learning.

Jonathan Kozol worries that artistry and imaginative creativity on the part of teachers are under serious assault. According to Kozol, "Scripted programs that are handed to the teachers and intended to keep children on an absolutely straight line to the destination of the next high stakes exam, leave little time for teachers to pay close attention to those children who won't give the answers we are told we must elicit from them or who, even more unpardonably, ignore our pre-planned questions and insist on asking better questions of their own" (2007, 50).

The arts are central to human learning and can serve as a foundation for education in many different settings. We live in a wonderfully culturally diverse society. By practicing culturally responsive education, we acknowledge, affirm, and celebrate diversity through many lenses, including differences in learning styles, age, class, levels of mental and physical ability, gender, race, and ethnicity. It is essential to model understanding of differences in our teaching and examine with students the richness and the challenges of a diverse society. "Learning to look through multiple perspectives, young people may be helped to build bridges among themselves; attending to a range of human stories, they may be provoked to heal and transform" (Greene 1992).

The arts provide a variety of ways for students to use what scientists and mathematicians refer to as *representational fluency*—the ability to use different symbolic systems to represent meaning. A concept that grew out of science and math disciplines, representational fluency "includes visualizing and conceptualizing transformation processes abstractly . . . transforming physical sensory data into symbolic representations and vice versa" (Lesh and Doerr 2003, 288). The arts provide opportunities for students to move between different representations of content. For students to create arts-based work, they must translate their understanding of content into new forms. They cannot translate without understanding. To move between languages and symbol systems to create new representations, students must draw on higher-order critical thinking skills, such as analysis and evaluation, leading to artistic creation. In poetry, students use words in new ways that are fresh and derive new meaning; in drama, they explore ideas through character, dramatic context, and multiple perspectives. Visual art harnesses the power of metaphor, and movement boils down concepts into their essence in ways that defy literal interpretation. Students translate information into new forms, blending ideas with their own unique perspectives, background experiences, voices, and intents.

Research continues to show how the arts are not mere window dressing in the public school setting; rather, when integrated properly into a curriculum, they can increase learning in key content areas. In a Ford-funded research study, *Voices from the Field: Investigating Teachers' Perspectives on the Relevance of Arts Integration in Their Classrooms* (Bellisario, Donovan, and Prendergast 2012), teachers were asked what benefits they discovered from arts integration practices in their classrooms. The data suggest that arts-integrated teaching:

- leads to deep learning and increased student engagement
- provides a variety of strategies for assessing content and expressing understanding
- is culturally responsive and creates learning that is relevant in students' lives
- engages students in creativity, innovation, and imagination
- renews teachers' commitment to teaching

Why should the arts be an integral part of teaching and learning?

- The arts address multiple learning styles, recognize multiple intelligences, and reach across cultures and languages to address the needs of every student.
- The arts promote analytical and critical-thinking skills and can be used to motivate learning and assess it.
- The arts address diversity by helping teachers create classrooms that teach to the needs of every student by presenting multiple perspectives, engaging parents and communities in learning, helping teachers critique schools as institutions, and instituting educational reform.
- The arts promote more democratic classrooms by expanding the number of languages able to be used in learning and by encouraging multiple perspectives.

Addressing Twenty-First-Century Skills through the Arts

"Being life ready means students leave high school with the grit and perseverance to tackle and achieve their goals by demonstrating personal actualization skills of self-awareness, self-management, social-awareness, responsible decision making, and relationship skills. Students who are life ready possess the growth mindset that empowers them to approach their future with confidence, to dream big and to achieve big."

—American Association of School Administrators (n.d., para. 1–2)

Educators and schools continue to face tough educational challenges. Amid the pressure to raise test scores, lower dropout rates, increase cognitive outcomes, and decrease disciplinary issues while effectively teaching to a wide range of abilities and ethnicities, there is increasing concern about how to best prepare today's students for success in a creative global economy.

Most educators would agree that there is a set of life and career skills and knowledge required for students to succeed:

- They must think critically and creatively.
- They must have organizational skills.
- They must be able to work well with others.
- They need to be self-confident, self-motivated, and self-disciplined.
- They need to understand and use mathematics, science, and technology.
- They need to be highly effective communicators.
- They need to understand and appreciate cultural diversity.

The practice of arts integration has proven to help students understand and practice these important skills. Arts integration employs strategies that build a strong platform for deep and meaningful learning. Students do not merely acquire information; they process and apply it. Observing, recording, organizing, collaborating, planning, practicing, revisiting, making predictions, experimenting, and communicating are among the life and career skills that are enhanced through arts integration (Burdette 2011). This is the kind of deep learning that students will need in the future. "More than ever, their health and well-being, success in the workplace, ability to construct identities and thrive in a pluralistic society, as well as their sense of agency as active citizens depends on gaining these skills" (Dunleavy and Milton 2008, 4).

Addressing Culturally Responsive Teaching through the Arts

"Utilizing the arts is key to creating inclusive classrooms. The arts—dance, media arts, music, theater, and visual arts—provide multiple ways for students to express themselves and their understanding of key content as well as the world around them. The arts provide an open door for students to share their authentic voice and their unique differences and contributions to the learning community. Inclusive classrooms include language, images, stories, and materials that reflect diversity and perspectives from groups or cultures that have been historically underrepresented."

—Lisa Donovan and Sarah Anderberg (2020)

Today's classrooms include students from a variety of unique backgrounds, experiences, and interests. As educators we must create a classroom culture that recognizes, responds to, and celebrates individual uniqueness in an equitable manner.

Culturally responsive teaching is a "pedagogy that recognizes the importance of including students' cultural references in all aspects of learning" (Ladson-Billings 1994). This is accomplished when teachers use varied strategies, resource materials, and approaches and respond to, acknowledge, and incorporate the cultural heritage of every student. When teachers do these things, they create an inclusive classroom that reflects the richness of the cultural diversity of the students.

There are many approaches to culturally responsive teaching, including diversifying the texts and materials used in teaching so that students see themselves in the curriculum and learn about others, creating "both mirrors and windows: mirrors to see ourselves reflected in the world, so we don't feel alone, and windows to see outside of our own lives, to recognize the humanity of other people" (Costello 2019).

The arts are inherently tied to expression and culture. When the arts are integrated into teaching and learning, creative thinking, observation, and analytical thought are put in motion. As a result, students are more engaged and learning is more relevant. Each student is recognized and valued for their uniqueness. The arts have the ability to create an environment that not only feels safe and welcoming but is student-centered. Students are proud of their backgrounds, languages, family traditions, and experiences, all of which, when recognized and shared, can build and strengthen a sense of cultural identity and a sense of self.

Each chapter of this book highlights strategies that, when implemented, help teachers create a classroom that encourages students' prior knowledge, builds relationships, and makes learning more contextual and relevant.

Addressing Universal Design for Learning and Differentiation through the Arts

"Our classrooms are diverse in many ways due to different experiences, socio-economic backgrounds, religion, race, gender and ability. Teaching toward the statistical average results in poor outcomes because the average student does not exist and therefore in reality we are teaching no one. However, when we acknowledge diversity and utilise the frameworks of UDL (see CAST 2019) and differentiation (see Tomlinson 2003) all students benefit. Consequently, UDL and differentiation are not only for students with disability, but provide benefit for everyone."

—Leanne Longfellow (2019, para. 1)

Universal Design for Learning (UDL) and differentiation have some similar approaches and some strategies that differ. It is important to distinguish and understand how and why they are similar and different to make decisions about how to design your lessons and how students experience the instruction.

Below are definitions of UDL and differentiation:

> UDL is an overarching approach focused on the inclusive design of the whole learning environment from the onset. UDL aims to ensure all students have full access to everything in the classroom, regardless of their needs and abilities. The approach supports self-directed learning and self-monitoring of progress. Universal Design for Learning invites educators to think about removing barriers from the curriculum and increasing access by diversifying teaching approaches (representation), increasing opportunities for students to engage with content in a variety of ways (engagement) and to provide students with many ways to express their understanding (expression). (New Zealand Ministry of Education, n.d.)

> Differentiation is a strategy aimed at addressing each student's individual level of readiness, interest, and learning profiles. The teacher modifies content and processes to address the needs of each student and directs students to specific activities to further their learning. (New Zealand Ministry of Education, n.d.)

These two strategies are interconnected because each does the following:

- Meets individual needs
- Gives all students access to the same high-quality content
- Supports highly engaging learning environments
- Provides multiple ways to develop and express knowledge and skills
- Assesses student progress during learning and adjusts as needed
- Occurs during independent practice (New Zealand Ministry of Education, n.d.)

How Does Arts Integration Support UDL and Differentiation?

Evidence suggests that instruction through the arts has a unique ability to reach children who might otherwise be left behind by traditional academic instruction. By integrating the arts with content instruction, teachers can effectively address the goals of UDL and differentiation to ensure that all learners reach chosen learning goals. The arts embody many paths to learning and inherently encompass multiple modalities through which students can show what they know. For example, kinesthetic learning is an essential aspect of creative movement, drama, and storytelling. The visual learning modality is engaged not only through the visual arts but also through gestures in storytelling and tableaux in drama. The auditory modality is used not only in music but also in storytelling, drama, and poetry.

Arts integration provides open-ended assignments, vocabulary development, self-paced activities, "sense-making" activities, and choice-based activities driven by student interest, all key strategies for UDL and differentiated instruction. For example, presenting an array of art-making supplies and encouraging students to think critically about which materials they will use to create a visual art piece requires students to use critical-thinking skills and provides opportunity for student choice. Working with English language learners to create a song about science content is an open-ended task that bolsters vocabulary development and helps students make sense of the curricular material.

To truly embrace UDL and differentiated instruction for all learners, teachers must continually assess student progress and understanding and adjust instruction accordingly. The arts provide flexible ways for students to demonstrate their knowledge at various stages of the learning process. For example, when students improvise scenes about mathematics content at the beginning of a unit of study, they demonstrate their prior knowledge of the content. The teacher can then plan instruction to meet students' needs based on the information learned through the scenes. The same improvisational activity performed over the course of the unit can be seen by both students and teacher as a formative assessment, showing what students have learned and demonstrating gaps in knowledge. Further instruction then can be adjusted to address student needs. When the dramatic activity is completed at the end of the unit, it can serve as a summative, performance-based assessment to show everything students have learned about the content.

The arts provide multiple, varied, open-ended ways for students to show what they have learned. A range of languages and symbol systems is available to students outside of the written expression they are expected to use in writing essays and taking tests. In the visual arts, students can use an endless array of materials to create pieces, in both 2D and 3D formats, and they can use line, color, texture, shape, and all the languages of visual art to show what they know about content. Students can use pitch, tone, rhythm, and melody in music to represent learning through voices, instruments, or simply clapping. Each student's product will be different. Students understand, through rubrics, checklists, and formative feedback, what they are expected to show they have learned, but the arts bring opportunities for multiple ways for students to demonstrate learning.

In the Classroom

Elementary teacher Sunie Caballero reports, "After nine years of teaching in the same elementary school that I attended as a child, I was beginning to feel bored. . . . Every day, I felt like a reading drill sergeant. I would faithfully administer 90 minutes of reading instruction plus an additional 30 to 90 minutes of interventions for the poor kiddos who were not reading at the expected level. Once I would suffer through the reading, I would then cram in 90 minutes of math instruction and, if possible, throw in some science, social studies, and writing. I would try to make my lesson plans creative and enriching, but I was frustrated, and so were my kids."

Caballero discovered that by integrating the arts, each student's strengths were accentuated. She had students use the reading material to create their own stories and illustrate them (storytelling and visual arts), create short improvisational skits based on the reading texts (drama), and make up songs and chants to summarize key facts (music and poetry). The curriculum was presented in a way that was innovative and interesting, because it engaged students and was relevant to them. Neither she nor her students were bored, and behavioral management issues decreased. In fact, the students looked forward to reading time, because they were personally engaged.

How to Use This Book

Begin to read this book wherever you feel comfortable. Pick a chapter that you are curious about or that resonates with you, or read the book cover to cover. The book begins with investigations of six art forms: storytelling, drama, poetry, music, visual arts, and creative movement. In these chapters, you will find basic information about the specific elements of each art form, along with investigations of basic assumptions and perceptions. Next, you will find specific examples and ideas for integrating the arts in the curriculum for grades K–12 as well as suggestions of how arts integration can reinforce culturally responsive teaching and social emotional learning. You also can successfully adapt the ideas in this book for learning in online and hybrid formats. Throughout these chapters, *In the Classroom* sections feature the voices of teachers who successfully integrated the arts into their classrooms. The final chapter shows you the nuts and bolts of creating a unit of study using arts integration.

Let this book work for you. Open it up and dive in. In the spirit of the stone dropped in the water, we hope you will begin by dropping even a small pebble into your classroom pool.

Observe what happens. Even if your stone is miniscule in size and the ripples that form are indeterminable waves, something is happening, and that something will continue to grow and expand and deepen. The learning environment is changing not only on the surface but underneath as well. Transformation is inevitable.

Step back and observe the classroom as students are engaged in an arts-integrated lesson. Consider how the arts activate different learning styles. For example, notice your students who thrive with movement, or who appreciate the challenge of spatial reasoning, or learn best through music. How does the atmosphere support the social-emotional wellness of your students?

Notice your own energy around teaching. What happens to you as a teacher when you integrate the arts in your unit on Westward Expansion, weather, or Shakespeare? What shifts for you when you allow students to become the creators, the inventors? How does your role change? Notice what happens in assessment. Are there improved results? Are students retaining information and becoming more successful? Has their confidence level risen?

Flight attendants often remind us that we should put on our oxygen masks first before helping others. However, as educators, sometimes we find this the most difficult challenge of all. It is easy to leave the needs of the teacher behind, administering everything possible to support our students. And thus, what is often overlooked is the impact integrating the arts has on teachers and teacher creativity.

"The arts can feed the inner lives of teachers, and the whole education enterprise depends on the quality of those inner lives. . . . Creativity involves drawing on sources from within, finding images, words, sounds, or movement inside oneself to express one's perceptions. This is what artists do. When teachers begin creating in the arts, they do the same. . . . They come to trust themselves as facilitators for children's learning and become powerful catalysts to evoke children's creativity" (Powell 1997). For both teachers and students, the arts have the power to renew energy, transform classrooms, and create innovative curriculum that inspires everyone to become lifelong learners.

We all want our students to be inspired lifelong learners, so we must create opportunities for learning to take place in an environment that allows for reflection, wonder, and creativity. Einstein once said, "It is, in fact, nothing short of a miracle that the modern methods of instruction have not entirely strangled the holy curiosity of inquiry" (Noddings 2006, 168). Students deserve every opportunity possible to become curious, imaginative, inspired learners. Drop the stone. Watch what happens.

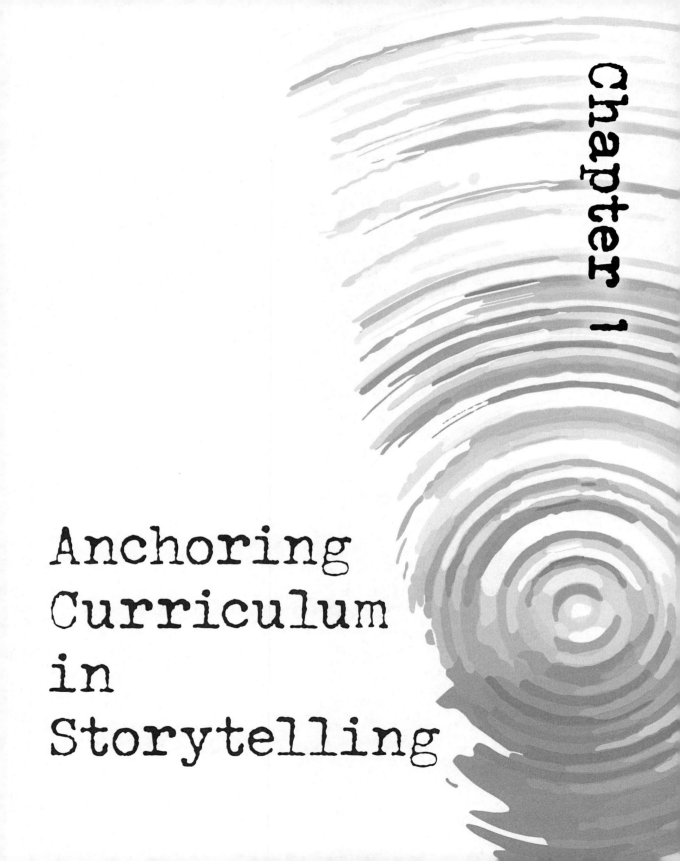

Anchoring Curriculum in Storytelling

Anchoring Curriculum in Storytelling

A good story transports you to another world, introduces you to fascinating characters, and invites you into their lives. Whether it's from a page, on a screen, or from personal experience, a good story has the power to connect and even change people. Storytelling in its most basic form is an art that has been around since the beginning of time. "Cultures from around the world have used storytelling as a way to preserve memories, share values and beliefs, instruct, and entertain. Long before written records, storytellers taught through an oral tradition" (Norfolk 2010).

Stories, whether fables, fairy tales, or stories from life, are one of the most basic ways to share knowledge, make sense of experiences, and see oneself in relation to others. In this chapter we explore the power of oral storytelling.

Stories can engage students while teaching at the same time. Bringing storytelling to your classroom not only links deeply to literacy but also communicates the power of the spoken word in connecting with others. Storytelling can build listening skills and model the art of communication (Story Arts 2000).

What Is Storytelling?

"Storytelling is the act of using language and gesture in colorful ways to create scenes in a sequence. A storyteller's cultural background and uniqueness shines through in the choice of words and gestures she/he chooses. Story time, in any form, is magical."

—Jeff Gere, Beth-Ann Kozlovich, and Daniel A. Kelin, II (2002)

We grow up telling and listening to stories in life. When we introduce storytelling in the classroom, we find that students have an internalized understanding of the structure of story, which helps them comprehend material embedded within a narrative (Landrum, Brakke, and McCarthy 2019). Language is shared, representing objects and ideas. By simply sharing a story from a summer vacation or what happened during the day, the storyteller can play with words and the subtleties of inflection and gesture. The storyteller shares their uniqueness and true identity with the listeners. Stories exercise the imagination and build literacy skills, serving as "flight simulators" in our minds as we make sense of our experiences (Oatley 2008). Stories not only trigger the imagination; research shows that our brains respond as if we really are experiencing the events in the story (Landrum, Brakke, and McCarthy 2019). This means that storytelling can help students develop background knowledge by engaging with story.

Storytelling, often thought of as an art form to be used only with young children, is a powerful learning tool for all ages, and when effectively implemented it can be successful with elementary through college-level students. For most of us, reading stories to children is a natural teaching technique. The elements of storytelling are familiar ones: interaction, words, action, story, and imagination (National Storytelling Network, n.d.). As teachers, we understand the power of hearing stories and reading stories to children. There's a magic that happens when you are swept away with the written word. A good story transports you into another world, introducing you to interesting characters and sharing insights into their lives. Stories can make you laugh and cry, and they have the power to change your feelings and perspectives.

> "Our brains love storytelling! Children—and adults—use stories to make sense of the world, and it's how we've taught passed on social skills and values to children for millennia."
>
> —Noah Teitelbaum (2021, para. 1)

Reading stories and telling stories are valuable teaching tools, but there are notable differences between the formats. Both strengthen literacy skills and directly connect to standards. Language development through narrative; knowledge of language structure; reflection; creativity; critical thinking; and spoken, written, and visual language are all enhanced through reading or telling a story.

Storytelling can create opportunities for students to share their own stories, as well as create invitations to step into the story world as they engage with a storyteller weaving a tale through voice, gesture, and interactive moments. Storytelling creates space for sharing our individual stories, providing opportunities for empathy, inclusiveness, and intersectionality. "These stories focus on affirming all children's identities, stories, and voices in our educational spaces" (Costello 2019, para. 25).

What Is the Difference between Reading a Story and Telling a Story?

A story read from a book does not change, but a storyteller constantly gauges the listeners' reactions to the performance, adjusting as the story goes on. When a story is read aloud from a book, the audience and the reader are focused on the story as it is written. The reader reads the text, and the audience looks at the pictures. The reader may read in the voices of the characters or add sound effects, but neither the reader nor the listeners influence the story itself.

Storytelling is powerful in ways that go beyond reading a story, and it benefits both the listener and the storyteller. Storytelling is powerful, because it is co-created and interactive. The storyteller, using narrative structure and mental imagery, communicates with an audience who are also using mental imagery, and together they create the story. A storyteller, using language and gestures, can create scenes in the mind of the listener. The listener, through imagination and visualization, is able to enhance the story and bring it to life. Reading a story aloud can accomplish this to some extent; however, the power of the storyteller to bring the story to life, through not only voice but body and emotion, makes the experience more personal. Just as hearing a live musical performance is an intense personal experience for the listener, listening to a story told by a storyteller provides an experience that becomes in itself more personal and intimate. For example, if a particular line or movement makes the audience laugh, the storyteller might repeat it or emphasize a similar line or gesture throughout the story. If the listeners are showing signs of losing interest, the storyteller might raise the energy level and make broader gestures, which in turn changes the listeners' focus. The storyteller can ask the listeners to participate by repeating lines or offer the listeners choices as to where the story should go. There is an interplay between the storyteller and the listeners that influences the story itself.

> "Good stories provide an opportunity to practice perspective-taking, the cognitive skill necessary for empathy."
>
> —Nicole Forsyth (2015, para. 5)

Why Does Storytelling Matter?

Storytelling is a powerful teaching and learning tool that develops the ability to imagine and visualize—skills that are integral to literacy development. When a student is asked to not only listen to a story but to summarize it and repeat it or retell it, learning increases. Visualization and imagination come into play, and memory is enhanced. Students' engagement in active listening is magnified. In addition, many teachers share that, much to their surprise, the most reluctant readers are eager to participate and share in the discussions about the story.

Storytelling benefits not only the listeners but the storyteller as well. The act of storytelling encourages active listening, builds analytical skills, and increases retention and comprehension. In other words, storytelling enhances literacy skills.

Telling an engaging story requires creating connection between the teller and the listener physically, mentally, and emotionally. Organization, sequencing skills, and creative thinking are all required. A student uses event knowledge to carry on discourse for multiple purposes: to frame language structures, learn and use new words, engage in fantasy play, make up stories, remember specific happenings, and form object categorization (Carr 2001).

Listeners hear and learn both familiar and new language patterns through storytelling. The act of thinking and reflecting occurs through storytelling. Both tellers and listeners have the opportunity to relate the story to their own lives and reflect and make connections. Storytelling, like other art forms, allows students who do not feel competent in reading or writing to excel through an art form that uses a combination of other language and expressive arts. A story is a powerful vehicle for sharing multiple perspectives and transmitting cultural values.

When creating a story, students use a wide range of communication strategies. In the process of creating a story, they apply knowledge of language structure and language conventions; conduct research; participate in reflective, creative, and critical thinking; and use spoken, written, and visual language. They use a combination of skills and processes to create a narrative linked to real or imagined events in a clear sequence.

Storytelling has a positive effect on the classroom community. When a story is told or retold, there is an immediate connection that is made between the storyteller and the audience. The audience becomes engaged in a shared experience that is quite different from hearing a story read aloud. Recent research has shown that "when one person tells a story and the other actively listens, their brains actually begin to synchronize" (Dooley 2010, para. 1).

Everyone has a story to tell, and sharing stories provides an effective vehicle for giving voice to a teacher and students. The act of sharing stories builds community, strengthens appreciation for one another, and allows many perspectives to be heard and considered.

"Many stories matter. Stories have been used to dispossess and to malign. But stories can also be used to empower and to humanize. Stories can break the dignity of people. But stories can also repair the broken dignity."

—Chimamanda Adichie (2016, para. 1)

When students tell their stories, it is their moment to have their voices honored. Stories provide a powerful vehicle for addressing issues such as bullying, racism, and bias around ability, gender, race, and sexual orientation. By hearing the voices of others, students build cultural bridges and have the opportunity to share their own personal stories. This can be powerful and insightful. Many points of view can be heard in a safe and respectful environment when students are able to tell their own and listen to others' personal stories. Stories can invite empathy and connection with characters and cultures who have different lived experiences from us, who have lived in different times, and who come from different traditions and experiences. Storytelling can build bridges and foster understanding in unparalleled ways in today's diverse classrooms.

Standards

Storytelling in College and Career Readiness Standards

The standards outline the expectation of young children to use a combination of drawing, dictating, and writing to narrate a single event where they recount two or more sequenced events, including some detail. Older students are expected to write and recount in narrative well-elaborated events, including details that describe action, thoughts, and feelings. All these standards are met through engagement in storytelling.

When teachers implement digital storytelling, students use a variety of technological and informational resources to create and gather information, thus addressing standards related to using technology to produce and publish writing.

The importance of building a strong and trusting classroom community cannot be underestimated. Storytelling helps establish a solid team environment, and the possibilities for successful teaching and learning dramatically increase through storytelling.

How to Become a Storyteller

Storytelling is a skill that can be easily learned, and it involves techniques that can be integrated into any subject or lesson. Storyteller Meg Lippert explains, "Teachers are often intimidated by the idea that they have to 'memorize' a story to tell it. Nothing is further from the truth. In fact, it is often possible to tell a short folktale having heard the story once, if the listener is picturing the story unfold in sequence. Then all the teacher has to do is retell the story as they 'watch' it unfold" (pers. comm.). Once we as teachers work through our own fears and develop confidence and a storytelling repertoire, it becomes much easier to share stories with students. Stories naturally build community. When we share stories with students, they are much more eager to continue to learn and tell new stories to practice their oral fluency, which is the bridge to effective reading and writing.

"In educational settings, we often share stories utlizing written words and illustrations. But oral tradition is still the most wide-spread form of human communication. By incorporating creative movement and vocalization to create a journey, children are able to live inside oral narratives in a new way."

—Rachel Costello (2019, para. 36)

Start with Personal Stories and Folktales

Anyone can become a good storyteller, because we all have stories to tell. One of the best ways to begin is with a story that is very familiar, such as a family or personal story. Personal stories are a good place to start because they quite naturally come from an oral tradition and often have never been written down. Most important, there is no one "right" way to tell a personal story. Tell about the time your brother dressed up as a ghost and scared you or how Aunt Mika made a spice cake with whole cloves instead of ground cloves and everyone got quite a bit of spice when they took the first bite!

If students have trouble thinking of a personal story, try asking questions like these:

- Have you ever laughed so hard you fell out of your chair?
- How did you learn to swim or ride a bike?
- Have you ever been really scared?
- Have you ever done something you are proud of?

- Do you have stories about your family, friends, or neighbors?

- Can you tell a story about a moment you had to make a decision?

If no events come to mind, having students listen to other stories will help stir up memories.

An easy next step is to focus on folktales, which also are from the oral tradition. Once you have learned the sequence of events, you can tell a story in your own words. There are many, many folktale collections and folktale picture books that provide excellent resources (see the list in Figure 1.1). Explore your school and/or public library (folktales are in section 398.2) and hunt for books written by storytellers. These sources also will include background information about the cultures from which the stories come. There are many newly published folktales and audio recordings of stories now available in bookstores. Listening to recordings of stories helps provide a feel for oral cadences and vocal possibilities.

Figure 1.1: A List of Stories to Get You Started

Resources for Finding Stories to Tell

- National Storytelling Network (**storynet.org**). Its mission is to "advance all forms of storytelling within the community through promotion, advocacy, and education."

- **Storyteller.net**. This site offers a robust set of articles, and opportunities to read and listen to stories and build storytelling skills.

Resources for Developing Stories to Tell

- "Oral History Resources," **www.storybug.net/links/oralhistory. html**. Links to a superb collection of online resources for teachers, including guides, lesson plans, and examples.

- StoryCorps, **storycorps.org**. Offers suggestions, including teacher guides, for developing questions and capturing people's stories.

To get started, explore the stories found in the resources listed in Figure 1.1. There is a diverse array of excellent choices for beginning student storytellers. When you and students become familiar with the patterns of these tales, you can easily use them to create your own stories.

Make the Story Your Own

Storytellers need to make stories their own. If there is a story that you like but find it doesn't quite meet your needs, try to seek out several versions and then create your own, using some of the strategies described by storyteller and former elementary school teacher Meg Lippert (2005):

- Identify the qualities of the characters and infuse your telling with these. Add dialogue, gestures, or movement to convey a sense of wiliness, sloth, or wisdom. If there are animal characters in the story, play with animal sounds and character voices.

- Many stories benefit from humor in word play, characterizations, or unexpected events. If there are places you can insert humorous elements, try them. They may become treasured moments.

- Remember the setting. This element is often missing from folktales in collections, yet it is important to share clues that will let listeners know where and when the story takes place. Just mentioning a palm tree or a blackberry bush may help them relax into the surroundings and join in the imagined story place.

- Amid all your tinkering with the story, remember the underlying message. Is it about overcoming pain, dealing with adversity, sustaining hope, or caring for others? After adjusting the story for these elements, ask yourself, *Did I retain the heart of the story?*

Getting Students to Tell Their Own Stories

Storytelling can be engaged using a book character mask. Credit: E. Shea, Newburyport, Massachusetts.

Leader Kevin Cordi of *Voices of Illusion: Youth Storytelling in California* strongly believes that the most important aspect of storytelling is for students to experience telling stories to one another. "The most important audience for students is themselves. I have watched how quickly a sense of group cohesion builds from not only youth telling stories, but youth listening to stories and from this exchange other youth build ideas for stories and begin loving them. In this environment, a sense of community grows;

a community that cares about each other and a community that shares with one another. There is a positive sense of value for the growth of not only a person's story but the person himself" (Norfolk 2010, 149).

Introductory Activity: Step-by-Step Process for Learning to Tell a Story

The following is storyteller Meg Lippert's easy-to-follow, step-by-step process to guide students to successfully tell their own stories. The story can be related to any content area: a folktale or fable, a historical event, a scientific process or concept (for example, how a caterpillar becomes a butterfly, the water cycle), or a series of math problems (for example, 10 cookies disappear in groups until they are all gone, cells multiply by splitting repeatedly).

- **Tell:** Tell a simple story to students, using voice and gesture to help the story come to life.

- **Retell:** Help students retell the story as a group, with volunteers adding parts in sequence. If students start retelling a story from a point in the middle of the story, respond with the following: "Yes, that is correct, and what happened before that?" Encourage students to add voice and gesture to make the story more engaging.

- **Review:** Review the story structure, listing the major elements of the story on the board. Go over the beginning, ending, and any key dialogue. When students know how the story starts and how it ends, the story will flow more fluently. Remind students to visualize the story and to describe what they "see" rather than focusing on the exact words of the story.

- **Tell to the Wall:** Have each student find a place in the classroom facing a wall. Tell students that when you give them a signal, they are to begin telling the story to the wall, as if they were telling it to another person. When they finish, discuss the experience. Ask: "Did you get stuck? Which parts flowed smoothly?" (Hamilton and Weiss 2005, 103).

- **Tell to a Partner:** Pair students up and ask partners to tell the stories to one another. If time is short, ask them to take turns, with one starting the story and telling halfway through and their partner telling the rest of the story.

- **Celebrate!** Within 30 minutes, students are storytellers. Encourage them to tell the story to their family and friends. Provide opportunities for them to tell the story to another class at their grade level or to younger children in the school. Remind them that when their families ask them, "What did you learn in school today?" they have a new story to tell. Have students keep a list of tales they know so they can begin to build a repertoire they can retell to share their learning and entertain themselves, their friends, and their families.

From Telling to Writing: Getting Students to Write Their Stories

It's a small step to go from students telling their stories to students writing their stories. To begin, make sure they have heard and can tell several stories with a traditional structure. With students, choose a familiar story and break it into components to identify the character qualities, the plot sequence, and the ending using *Making a Story Structure* (Figure 1.2). When students understand this story structure, have them follow

Figure 1.2 Making a Story Structure

Making a Story

1. Who is your story about?

   - What kind of person/animal is your character?

   - How big or small is your character?

   - What does your character look like?

   - What is your character wearing?

   - What does your character like?

   - What does your character want or need?

   - What is your character afraid of?

   - What is your character's name?

2. How does your character get what they want or need? Try out different scenarios and see what is the most interesting and imaginative.

3. What is the title of your story? Make a list of several ideas and then choose one.

the structure to write their own stories based on characters they create. This can be a prewriting activity that leads to them writing more complete and more clearly structured stories (Meg Lippert, pers. comm.).

Storytelling across the Curriculum

Once students are familiar and comfortable with storytelling, try some of these simple storytelling ideas that can be used at any grade level.

Storytelling in English Language Arts

Storytelling is a natural fit in language arts classrooms. You can work with folktales, myths, and other stories told over time to tell and retell. "Storytelling teaches listening. It models fine use of oral language. It models plot, sequencing, characterization, the many literary devices you wish to convey" (MacDonald 1994).

There are endless possibilities for stories to explore. Consider the wide range of stories that fall within the category of folktales, including trickster tales, fairy tales, porquoi, legends, fables, myths, and so on.

Storytelling in Social Studies

Storytelling can bring history to life for students by inviting them to connect with historical characters, small moments, and specific places. For example, storyteller Beth Horner investigates the impact of the Civil War on families of soldiers through stories based on the use of primary source documents including photographs and letter excerpts. She brings historical characters to life and explores historical events by zooming into a particular moment through a story told through one person's perspective, examining specific moments in detail (Stenson and Norfolk 2012, 89).

She describes her process: "Dates and places are important, but small moments bring it home to the heart of the listener. A 'drop away moment' is a moment in the story when all else falls away from the story and the listener's mind accepts that one instant in time and the image associated with it. The story zooms in like a camera lens so that nothing else is seen or experienced by the listener but that one moment. My intent is for the listener to linger over that living, breathing moment, as if frozen in time, and to take the resulting image into [their] heart" (as cited in Stenson and Norfolk 2012, 93).

Storytelling in Science

Storytelling can help students grasp complicated scientific concepts and processes by requiring them to break the content down and then reassemble it in sequence. Here are some stories and experiments that work well together.

- **Scientific method:** Explore the elements of the scientific method through a story, expanding on the processes of observation, problem statement, and idea generation. Experiments and experimental design can be explored through a story about a scientist who carries out a skillfully planned, carefully organized, and cleverly conducted experiment.

- **Spiders:** Tell a spider story, such as "Anansi and the Moss-Covered Rock" or "Why the Spider Has a Small Waist." Then have students research or read how spiders build webs and find food and tell what they have learned through stories.

- **Metamorphosis, frogs:** Tell a frog story, such as "How the Frog Lost Its Tail." Then have students learn about metamorphosis from egg to tadpole to adult frog and tell stories to show what they know.

- **Chemical change, fire:** Tell "The Snooks Family" or "Twist-Mouth Family," both stories of how family members have trouble blowing out candles. Experiment with mixing baking soda and vinegar to form carbon dioxide, which will extinguish a lighted candle, and have students create stories about the process.

- **Astronomy:** Share with students American Indian stories about why we have day and night or seasons before they learn the scientific explanations. Then have them create their own stories to explain scientific phenomena (Sima 2012).

Challenge students to create stories that personify scientific ideas (for example, organisms or chemical or biological processes). Use stories to build toward complex ideas, providing students with a frame to hold scientific ideas (Homann 2017).

Invite students to tell stories about scientists, their work and struggles, particular scientific investigations, or behind-the-scenes experiences of the scientific topic. One useful website is *The Story Behind the Science* (**www.storybehindthescience.org**).

Storytelling in Mathematics

Sometimes students have difficulty understanding a concept in mathematics, and even using concrete examples and manipulatives does not seem to help. How can teachers supplement the use of manipulatives to help boost students' understanding in mathematics? Zemelman, Daniels, and Hyde recommend that students discuss, write, read, and listen to mathematical ideas to deepen their understanding of difficult concepts (1998). Using storytelling as a catalyst for mathematics instruction is one enjoyable and versatile method of doing this, because storytelling appeals to students' imaginations and emotions and helps make learning more meaningful. When students listen to stories, they create mental images that belong to them, connecting the content to something personally significant.

Storytelling engages students in problem solving that invites them into the story world, creating a sense of relevance, connection, and context. Math matters when it's placed in a particular story with characters we care about and a setting, situation, and problem to be solved. You can investigate existing stories for math linked to the story, tell the stories to students, and invite them to "stop and figure" once the problem has been laid out, thereby helping them become part of the story. Students can create robust stories that bring word problems to life in imaginative ways, building plot on key mathematical keys and outcomes.

In the Classroom

Storytelling helps students deepen their concept of place value by connecting it to an experience. One example comes from Mary Barr Goral and Cindy Meyers Gnadinger (2006), elementary math teachers, who, in the interest of helping their students understand place value, made up a story called "Queen Arithma's Party"—a story about a queen who was throwing a big party and needed to organize hundreds of invitations. Although the experience was a fantasy story, the main character had a real problem that needed to be solved. And using place value helped solve the problem. Students had to work in groups to bundle the invitations into groups of hundreds, tens, and ones to figure out how many invitations there were. Listening to the story and participating in problem solving related to the story helped reinforce the concept and met the standard.

Have students tell the story of an equation, bringing "story problems" to life. Students also can create stories based on graphs and charts. Ask, "What story do the data tell?" For geometry, have students create stories about various shapes meeting one another. Ask students questions such as "What happens when a trapezoid meets a rectangle? What do they have in common? What conflict might they have?" Telling stories is a natural way to reinforce patterning. Most stories have a sequential pattern to them. Have students identify and represent these patterns visually or mathematically.

Storytelling and Visual Arts

Invite students to work from a photograph, political cartoon, or painting to draw out details to spark a story. Students also could create visual effects to go with their storytelling (sets, props, posters, and so on). Moving between different "languages" stimulates students to use analysis, synthesis, and evaluation—the highest levels of thinking.

In the Classroom

Visual arts teacher Jessica Holloway uses storytelling in her classes to create context and deeper meaning for art projects. For example, in her fifth-grade classes, she tells the story *Tunjur! Tunjur! Tunjur! A Palestinian Folktale* (MacDonald 2006) about a childless woman who prays to Allah for progeny and is rewarded with a mischievous little cooking pot with human attributes. The story gives context to the ceramic face jugs that Holloway has her students make. Students sketch facial expressions and create a pot expression in clay. As a culminating activity, students create tags to tell viewers what their pot's "mouth is full of," just like the story. The story helps students imagine which materials in a mouth would result in which face.

Storytelling and Music

A ballad is a story poem with a strong rhyme and rhythm. Many of them focus on tales from history. Have students listen to a few ballads and then try creating a group ballad about their content-area learning.

Digital Storytelling

Digital storytelling combines the art of storytelling with a variety of digital multimedia such as images, audio, and video. Digital stories bring together some mixture of digital graphics, text, recorded audio narration, video, and music to present narratives. As with traditional storytelling, digital stories revolve around a chosen theme and particular viewpoint. The stories are typically only a few minutes long and include personal tales, retellings of historical events, or information on a particular subject.

Before students are able to create their own digital stories, they need to view several examples. Once they have experienced learning new material through this multimedia venue, they are much more apt to create their own. Several websites inform and instruct educators on the nuances of digital storytelling (see Appendix D: Recommended Resources).

In all these areas, use existing stories told and retold in interactive ways that engage students. Or have students develop and tell their own stories, researching, writing, and performing them around topics and weaving facts into their stories. Students can conduct interviews with family and community members and share those stories through storytelling. They can bring creative voice and choice to the storytelling process as they introduce a variety of characters and settings, use a narrator, and engage the listeners' ideas and responses as the story unfolds. Stories can be told by a single teller or told by a group, with each member playing a different role in the telling. Storytelling is a flexible, engaging strategy that can be used across curricular areas.

Concluding Thoughts

Many claim that storytelling is the heart and soul of education. It allows diverse points of view to be presented, provides a place for personal histories and prior experiences to be shared, and allows students with a wide range of linguistic abilities and ethnic backgrounds to come together and learn.

All people have a basic need to share stories. Stories are a way to organize experiences and record important occurrences. And stories are of great significance in language and literacy development, especially when considering the increased linguistic and cultural diversity of classrooms today (Koki 1998).

For some students, once a story is told, capturing the story in writing becomes much easier. Listeners also benefit through encountering both familiar and new language patterns. Hearing language is the first step in re-creating it, both orally and in written form.

Stories are one of the most effective ways, at any level of schooling, to pass on information. Historical events remain in a student's mind when communicated by a narrative. The ways of other cultures, both ancient and living, acquire honor in story. The facts about how plants and animals develop, how numbers work, or how government policy influences history—any topic, for that matter—can be incorporated into story form and made more memorable if the listener takes the story to heart (Dudding 2005).

This ancient art form can inspire students of all grade levels. Through storytelling we can address connections to perspectives across society, utilize their power in the classroom, and serve increasingly diverse student populations most effectively.

Tom Lee telling a story prompted by an illustration from the Indian epic *Ramayana*. (www.tomleestoryteller.net/)
Photo credit: Craig Norton.

Reflection

1. Select one planned lesson you intend to use in the next week. How can you integrate storytelling into that lesson?

2. How might you use storytelling to bring multiple perspectives and diverse voices into your curriculum?

3. Observe students as they tell their stories. What did you notice about their levels of motivation and engagement? Why do you think this is?

The Power of Dramatic Inquiry

The Power of Dramatic Inquiry

What Is Drama?

When you hear the word *drama*, what do you think of? Often teachers initially confuse drama with theater, envisioning a staged performance with lights, costumes, and sets. They imagine students as actors memorizing lines. Too often, they believe that they cannot bring this work into their classrooms. While dramatic work can lead to this kind of performance, process drama offers a whole different experience in educational settings. Theater is focused on developing a final product for an audience. Drama, on the other hand, is focused on the process of exploration—on the growth and imagination of its participants. It uses improvisation, or acting choices that unfold in the moment, rather than memorizing scripts. Drama is about learning rather than putting on a polished performance. Focusing on the dramatic investigation is the main goal of dramatic inquiry—investigation of ideas, stories, historical moments, scientific discoveries, and so on.

By becoming characters, creating and exploring a particular context or situation, students have a sense of entering into the story itself, which creates a deeper connection to the work and provides opportunities to explore character, context, and perspective.

Former middle school teacher, drama educator, and researcher Jeffrey Wilhelm defines drama strategies as exploring scenarios where students "imagine to learn" (Wilhelm and Edmiston 1998). Cecily O'Neill describes drama as "a dramatic 'elsewhere,' a fictional world, which will be inhabited for the insights, interpretations, and understandings it may yield" (1995, 12). Drama also can be thought of as the use of body, voice, and imagination to explore the stories of our world (Donovan 2005). Thinking of drama in this way provides opportunities for students to use their imaginations to enter into curriculum in new ways and to explore ideas from a range of vantage points. In drama integration, the teacher learns side-by-side with students as they explore new landscapes of learning.

"Teachers can promote learning in the classroom with a range of various drama activities which can encourage, among others, the *development of speaking, listening and comprehension skills*. These skills can be acquired by using a text through role playing, interacting with others, visualizing events, concepts, and information, and dramatizing the experiences of fictional and real-life characters."

—iDevelop Teacher Training (2019, para. 3)

Why Does Drama Matter?

"The purpose of playing, whose end, both at first and now, was and is, to hold, as 'twere, the mirror up to nature."

—Hamlet (Shakespeare)

Research has shown that engagement in drama can deepen comprehension, bolster language skills, and develop awareness of and sensitivity to multiple perspectives (Wilhelm 2007). It can support the development of communication fluency and increase motivation for learning.

Drama, by its nature, provides the possibility to examine life's most complex issues. The process serves as a hands-on tool for exploring complex social issues, relationships, and the nature of cause and effect. It provides the opportunity to "try on" different roles and courses of action to see how perspective and personal choice affect circumstance in a controlled laboratory setting. The goal of the work is not to achieve one right solution, but rather to try many different potential approaches to investigate a story, issue, or moment. In this way, students can fully analyze the nuances of the situation. By placing students inside a moment or event, they are able to see their role in its outcome, understand the views of others, and learn how they might have an impact. Process drama provides a window to understanding how relationships of power work and requires participants to consider vantage points different from their own.

Engagement

A common complaint of students is education's lack of relevance to their lives: "Why do I have to know this?" Research shows that for students who drop out of school, the disconnect begins as early as fourth grade (Harpaz 2009). There is so much content to be learned, and so many skills to be developed, that too often the real-world connections and engagement that students need are put in the "only if we have time" category. The integration of drama in the classroom can help build the bridge between content knowledge, skills, and relevance to students' lives.

Students can work with different dramatic elements to bring stories to life, exploring a wide variety of roles and characters in interesting settings and situations, encountering conflicts that create dramatic tension. Timing and use of space can activate drama to create a felt sense of here and now for moments, scenes, and processes across the curriculum. By illuminating facets of students that teachers were unaware of, drama provides experiences in the classroom that allow each student to find their own voice (Gallas 1991; McCaslin 2000). Engagement in drama appeals to a variety of learning styles, allowing students to connect with the work according to how they learn. In the last few decades, much of what the arts can accomplish has been fueled by Howard Gardner's work on multiple intelligences. Gardner proposes that there are nine kinds of intelligence, or ways of learning: linguistic, logical-mathematical, spatial, kinesthetic, musical, interpersonal, intrapersonal, existentialistic, and naturalistic (Gardner 1983). Current thinking in brain research and the call for supporting variable learners support the use of multiple ways of accessing curriculum, engaging with content, and representing understanding (Center for Applied Special Technology n.d.). Most curricula focus on learning that appeals to the first two intelligences: linguistic and logical-mathematical. The arts span all these intelligences and, as a result, provide a useful method for tapping into students' diverse learning styles. Gardner's work encourages an expanded view of the arts and their relationship to education (McCaslin 2000).

> "Through immersive drama-based experiences, students practice life skills, from collaboration to critical thinking to creative problem-solving."
>
> —Daniel A. Kelin (2020, para. 3)

Standards

Drama in College and Career Readiness Standards

Participation in drama, both as an actor and an active audience member, addresses many of the listening and speaking standards, such as collaboration with diverse partners, building on others' ideas, adapting speech to a variety of contexts, and evaluating a speaker's point of view. By assuming a dramatic role, students view a text from the inside out and take on many vantage points, thus analyzing the structure of texts, assessing how point of view or purpose shapes a text, making logical inferences from text, determining central ideas or themes, and analyzing how individuals, events, and ideas develop and interact over the course of a text.

One of the benefits of drama in the classroom is the development of students' voices. Often students lack confidence in expressing who they are. By exploring ideas of characters different from themselves, students locate their own ideas, values, and belief systems. They are no longer passive and accepting of the text and information they are being presented with. Instead, they learn to question, research, discover, and build their own opinions. In their investigations of a range of characters, contexts, and stories, students develop the ability to be aware of their own voice as well as the voices of others. They consider how voice works in relationship with others. And they have the opportunity to develop and expand modes of expression and communication (Donovan 2005).

As Rachel Mattson notes, "The core of this work lies in the process of discovering ideas, not in the preparation for any kind of public presentation" (2008, 102). Maxine Greene's writings (1978) advocate providing students with access to the arts to energize them to "wide-awakeness." Engaging with art can lead to questioning of how we relate to the world.

In the Classroom

What does integrated drama look like in the classroom? Tacoma, Washington, middle school science teacher Kalee Alexander uses drama to move beyond memorization to help her students grasp difficult concepts. After her students view cells under a microscope, Alexander uses dramatic techniques to have them imagine themselves as organelles and the whole classroom as a cell. Students must consider the organelles' dynamic structures and their work within cell structures. Students construct deeper knowledge through this exploration, and Alexander is better able to dispel misconceptions as students work. She notes, "It's not enough just to know the vocabulary. It's more to understand what that vocabulary means, and one way we can understand what something means is by looking at it through many different lenses. So in an attempt . . . to make an organelle—which is very abstract— more concrete, I thought it would be very effective to act it. And it gives [students] inspiration" (Bellisario, Donovan, and Prendergast 2011).

Exploring Multiple Perspectives

A well-rounded education must include elements that promote an understanding of students' own backgrounds and cultures and awareness that theirs is not the only perspective. Asking students to reflect on their backgrounds and what makes them who they are develops an awareness of where they come from. Often the sense of what has influenced them is so ingrained that they have lost the ability to see it without looking for it (Banks 1994; McIntosh 1990). This "monocultural" perspective leaves students thinking that there is one cultural system that everyone is part of. This notion blocks students from understanding others who are different from them. As McIntosh notes, "There is no culturally unmarked person" (1990, 3).

Participating in drama can allow students the opportunity to inhabit other perspectives, develop empathy, and develop the ability to understand the many vantage points that come into play in any situation. As students imagine they are characters and envision themselves in specific environments and circumstances, they can act out different choices based on their characters' frames of reference. Realizing that there are perspectives other than one's own is critical to success in a world that is ever more diverse and complex.

Drama integration can encourage cultural grounding for students and sensitize them to an awareness of otherness. This knowledge, once unearthed, creates an awareness of how powerfully their unique perspectives and backgrounds influence their responses to life issues. Students need to be aware that they carry assumptions about the world with them. Exploring their own set of assumptions provides students with a basis for understanding their own socio-cultural perspectives. Rachel Mattson (2008), reflecting on integrating drama in the study of history, notes that process drama "also has the power to raise the stakes of critical historical analysis for young people, provoking students' curiosity and inviting an embodied form of critical primary document analysis" (103).

Describing the power of dramatic role-play, Timothy Doherty says, "Students are . . . offered the chance through improvised role-plays to rehearse, 'inhabit,' and 'voice' perspectives. Role-plays offer the possibility of sensitizing students to both their limits and capacities for understanding unfamiliar points of view" (1996, 157).

This investigation of what informs the decisions of a particular character leads to skills in empathy and understanding human behavior that foster better collaboration and leadership development. Teacher Brenda Rosler noticed in an exploration of historical content in her fifth-grade classroom that some students' involvement "went beyond mere engagement, as they became active decision makers and leaders in the drama" (2008, 267).

Exploration of Ideas

Dramatic work activates students' thinking processes. It requires that knowledge and information be transformed. Students use their understanding of a situation and a character to create new ground in a dramatic situation. They play with a fictional set of circumstances, investigating a diverse range of possibilities for human behavior. Drama develops students' ability to think divergently, imagine possibilities, and test ways of responding to the world that equip them for success that we can't yet imagine. Nellie McCaslin, in discussing the creative influence of drama, notes, "Creativity is the act of repatterning the known world into meaningful new configurations" (2000, 25).

Drama magnifies and explores sensitive issues by using metaphor to understand complex concepts (Boal 1995; Goldberg and Phillips 1995; Parsons and Blocker 1993; Schutzman and Cohen-Cruz 1994). It provides a lens for looking at problems and uncovering fresh perspectives.

Because drama can isolate situations and magnify moments and ideas, it provides the opportunity to tease out nuances of complex issues and concepts. It can provide distance, a safe space within which one can walk amid the pieces of a complex puzzle, reflect, and consider while keeping emotion and personal agenda at bay. Teacher Kate DePalo notes, "I have already noticed that my classes are collaborating on a different level. They are dissecting information through exploration and as a result have been extremely intuitive, thoughtful, and engaged. I have found that through drama my students are building relationships and making connections with the material" (pers. comm.).

Communication Fluency

Drama work calls on students to use their full range of physical expression, explore the nuances of verbal and nonverbal communication, and become astute observers. Drama requires that students communicate both with words and without, developing an awareness of context and perspective and how this affects communication—in other words, how things are communicated and how they are received.

Think about how much there is to learn about effective communication. In addition to words, incorporating the details of speech that hold information—pauses, stutters, half-statements—adds unspoken meaning. Theater artist Normie Noel makes the point that it is important to consider all these nuances, because a quiet moment, pause, or false start can communicate more than a full sentence. The *way* in which we communicate, not just what we say, is loaded with meaning (pers. comm.). This knowledge is invaluable to students who are learning how to communicate effectively, and that language is informed by context, inflection, and nonverbal communication.

Supporting Reading Comprehension

Research has shown that successful reading requires being able to enter into the world of the story. Drama can bolster students' comprehension of a story by allowing them to explore the story from inside and physically embodying the story and its characters. When participating in drama, students create the meaning of the text through their words, both written and spoken; kinesthetically through the motion and positioning of their bodies; visually through their stance and observation of others; emotionally through their feelings, often expressed in gesture, music, or writing; intrapersonally as they reflect; and interpersonally as they create shared meanings by reacting and responding to the dramatic actions of others (Wilhelm 2007).

This kind of learning moves beyond the simple understanding of a story. Rather, as David Booth says, "Drama encourages children not to be satisfied with immediate, simplistic solutions but to keep exploring, peeling away the layers that cloud the meaning; it can help develop the 'what if' element that must be brought to print if true reading is to occur" (as cited in Wilhelm and Edmiston 1998, 37). This kind of engagement brings deeper comprehension and connections to students' real lives. Because they have experienced a text in a multisensory way—physically, emotionally, and visually—their learning is deeper and retention is longer.

Unique connections and impressions of a story can provide a jumping-off point for how we choose to understand a story. Through drama we can explore the places where the listener connects with the story world. Jeffrey Wilhelm says, "As a teacher, I invite students to imagine together, actively depicting characters, forces, or ideas, and to interact in these roles. An enactment may be cast in the past, the present, or the future, but always happens in the 'now of time.' This is relevant in education because through enactments, you can highlight and teach strategies of reading and learning, and help students create interpretations of text that reverberate with artistic, aesthetic, and metaphoric meanings" (Wilhelm and Edmiston 1998, 8). These dramas draw on what students know from prior knowledge and allow them to make sense of the text they are reading.

> "Teachers were able to act more like facilitators and leaders than guardians of knowledge. Students were able to discover for themselves instead of being told what to look for in a text; they found the importance, beauty, pain, and nuances themselves."
>
> —Sara Ranzau and Ashley Thomas (2016)

What is created in an enactment must fit what students know from the text and the world. Dramatic enactments make hidden processes of reading and learning visible, manipulatable, and open to evaluation and revision (Wilhelm 2007). Wilhelm's research demonstrated the role of dramatic enactments in helping students "to 'take on the participant stance' to participate in and visualize textual worlds, enlivening their engagement with text, and assisting them in creating meaning with text" (Beach et al. 2002, 164).

Critical Literacy: Investigating Texts

The most powerful effect of drama is the ability to engage students in imagining themselves in a role. Each role has a particular lens or frame of reference through which the world is seen. Donning the dramatic lens allows students to be comfortable moving between perspectives—their own and that of others. Looking at the same situation through these various lenses prompts an understanding that there are many interpretations of a particular story. Asking students then to consider who is telling the story creates a heightened awareness and questioning of texts. Wilhelm and Edmiston write that drama provides "a way of making meaning of the world by learning to look inward to define the self; to imagine and enter the selfhood and perspectives of others; and . . . to look outward to critically read and converse with the world, open always to change and transformation and to working toward these transformations" (1998, 149).

The process of dramatic inquiry allows us to unpack and explore various aspects of the story. Not only does this deepen comprehension; it prompts the development of critical literacy, where texts are not accepted at face value but explored from a variety of access points. We often assume there is one interpretation of a story. This is, of course, not true, and the story will change based on the vantage point from which it's told. A dramatic investigation of a story might probe these questions:

- From whose perspective is the story told?
- Who are the voices represented?
- Which voices are missing?
- What are the relationships between characters?
- What is the context of the story?
- What choices are made by each character and why?

In the language arts classroom, this kind of exploration will bring a heightened sense of characters' inner worlds and choices. In social studies, it could lead to a questioning of who's telling the story and a consideration of how the story might be represented differently if told by another character.

We know that students are invited to explore multiple perspectives by stepping into the shoes of a particular character and context. Dramatic exploration creates opportunities for our students to be exposed to perspectives that are different from our own, fostering empathy and awareness that ours is not the only vantage point.

Drama allows students to experience something at many levels—aesthetically, emotionally, intellectually, and analytically. It develops the ability to tune in, not just receive, activating students to think, rethink, analyze, evaluate, and identify the relevance of a text to their lives. What better way to develop literacy than by entering the world of the text, becoming the characters you are reading about, and thus understanding why they make the choices they do? Dramatic enactment can serve to deepen reading skills in the traditional sense, including comprehension and the implications for critical literacy where students learn to question texts and assumptions and not accept a text as the truth.

Student teachers collaborating with a seasoned educator who integrates the arts into her classroom shared their experiences of using drama in the exploration of novels. They described how drama integration "allowed the students to see novels in a new way, which increased their critical thinking skills and engagement. Students more quickly discovered emotions of the characters, questioned character motivations, and realized what they may have missed during the reading." Students created tableaux exploring major events and social positioning of characters in the novel "so they could process, analyze, and discuss the social structures and power changes within a novel. The tableau activity has served as an excellent way for students to think carefully about the most important events within a novel, summarize the story, and learn how to work together." The work was documented through photographs, and the teachers noted, "Students were surprised at how each group saw characters differently, yet no group was wrong. The activity helped the students realize the power structure of a novel changes throughout the entire story." Later on in the exploration, a role-play depicting a town hall meeting allowed students to investigate ideas of character motivation. "When students imagine themselves as Boo Radley or Tom Robinson, instead of seeing the story only from Scout's point of view, they are able to create a life for the town, contemplate their own views of life, and develop empathy for characters. The writing that students create as they attempt to make inferences and embody their chosen character often reveals truths or ideas to them that they might not discover in class discussion. Their voice becomes stronger as they imagine themselves as that character and attempt to imitate the voices of Boo or Tom." This exploration moved beyond words of a text and led to the opportunity to bring forward student questions and individual interpretation (Ranzau and Thomas, 2016).

> "The theater is like a gym for empathy. It's where we can go to build up the muscles of compassion, the practice of listening and understanding and engaging with people that are not just like ourselves."
>
> —Bill English (n.d.)

Supporting English Language Learners

How often have you had English language learners who struggle to learn because they are not yet comfortable with English? Through drama, students are provided opportunities that simulate reality so language exploration and learning occur in context and can be framed in a safe environment where risk taking is supported. Culturally responsive strategies, such as reader's theater, tableau, improvisation, visualization, and pantomime, provide multiple points of access at different levels of language learning. Physical expression, vocal variety, spoken word, and writing to explore the academic language of social studies respond to contextual clues, relationship and circumstance, and language as a way to engage socially. Sue Rieg and Kelli Paquett note, "Besides being 'fun' learning experiences for children, drama and movement have been proven to assist with developing decoding skills, fluency, vocabulary, syntactic knowledge, discourse knowledge, and metacognitive thinking" (2009, 148). Drama not only "naturally integrate[s] the basic language skills, but drama also integrates the verbal and non-verbal aspects of communication, attends to the cognitive and affective domains, fosters awareness of self and others, builds learner autonomy, ownership and self-esteem, and brings to life fully contextualized, fluent classroom interaction in the target language through its focus on meaning and exploratory learning under the instructor's supervision and facilitation" (Bataineh and Salah 2017).

Introductory Activity: Tableaux

Asking students to portray a concept without using words will provide a challenge and stretch their thinking. Give students a word or concept and have them use their bodies to represent that concept visually in a still picture, or tableau. Younger students can create shapes for concrete ideas such as inanimate objects and animals. Older students can tackle more abstract concepts such as balanced equations (mathematics), democracy (social studies), oxymoron (literature), or velocity (science). This activity can be done anywhere, anytime, with no preparation or materials.

1. **Create tableaux:** Give students a concept or vocabulary word and tell them they must use their bodies to create still shapes that represent that idea. Ask students to experiment with using different levels (placing their bodies in different positions at low, medium, and high levels) to make the image interesting. Once students have successfully explored the given concepts in single sculptures, you can move on to group tableaux that are more complex and show relationships between characters. Each group should identify a sculptor, and the rest of the group will be the "clay" (Boal 2002).

2. **Gallery walk:** Once students create their tableaux, you can ask them to create captions or titles for their images. This prompts students to move between image and text, which draws out new ideas. Have students decide whether they will reveal their captions before, during, or after the presentation of images to viewers (each choice will yield a different result).

   Ask the class to imagine they are in a sculpture gallery and have a "gallery walk" in which each tableau is viewed as a sculpture. As the students examine each tableau, ask them to name aloud what they think is being depicted. Keep a list of the words students suggest and discuss them later in relationship to the actual word. After the vocabulary word being portrayed is either identified or shared with the group, ask the creators to discuss their creative process and what choices they made in composing their image.

3. **Tapping in:** After students create and view a tableau, have an audience member "tap" a character or object to life. Ask the sculpted figure to share in a line or two what they might be thinking. By "tapping" characters/ideas/objects to life, the inner thinking process of a figure is revealed.

4. **Slideshow:** Move from vocabulary words to stories or sequenced concepts by asking students to create a series of tableaux to tell a story, as in a slideshow, where one image is shown right after the next. Each tableau should capture a snapshot of a moment in time. You can ask students who are viewing to close their eyes between each image by saying "Curtains down" (eyes shut) and "Curtains up" (eyes open). This allows the groups who are creating an image to prepare their sculpture so the viewers see only the completed image.

Tableaux: Curriculum Connections

Tableaux can be used flexibly across content areas. In mathematics, students can create tableaux of where polygons appear in the world. Their peers then guess both the items being portrayed and the contexts for the shapes. In science, students can create tableaux of mitosis and meiosis in a series of images like a slideshow that reveals how cells divide. Each tableau "slide" has a caption that describes the moment. In social studies, students can depict a moment that might have occurred during the signing of the Constitution, and historical figures are tapped to life, each saying a line that reveals their inner thinking.

Drama Strategies

Once students are comfortable with creating tableaux, introduce new dramatic strategies for learning curricular content. Give students a starting place, such as a specific moment in history or literature, the beginning of a scientific process, or the point in a mathematical problem at which they must make a choice about how to proceed. Introducing a scenario for students to explore can trigger a rich investigation framed by the characters, situation, context, and time period. Students bring the details to life through these strategies as the drama unfolds, allowing them to explore stories from the inside out.

Pantomime

"Pantomime is the art of conveying ideas without words" (McCaslin 2000, 71). Ask students to tell a story or show a concept through movement without using words. They can capture action, relationships, and the progression of a story without worrying about dialogue. Communicating ideas nonverbally will require students to think differently about the concepts they are portraying.

Improvisation

In improvisation students build dramatic scenes by creating the drama in the moment, without reading from a script. Give students characters, a location, and a time, and tell them to pretend they are the characters and let the drama unfold spontaneously.

This allows students to bring stories, historical moments, and concepts to life by applying their understanding of story, character, and motivation in their own language. This leads students to draw more fully on comprehension skills as they bring their understanding of a story into the improvised moment.

Mantle of the Expert

Mantle of the Expert, developed by drama educator Dorothy Heathcote, invites students to imagine that they are experts in the field being studied. Give students a role, such as a biologist who studies cell division or an expert on the Civil Rights movement, and have the other students interview the "expert." This encourages students to take on a particular role and specific lens, which then deepens the research or investigation that is taking place. "The students inhabit their roles as experts in the enterprise with increasing conviction, complexity, and truth" (Heathcote and Bolton 1995, viii).

Monologue

A monologue is a moment in a play or story in which a character speaks without interruption. This can be an internal monologue in which the character is speaking to themselves (soliloquy), or the monologue could be addressed to another character or to the audience. Have students select a character from history, literature, or a newspaper story and create a monologue, focusing on an issue that this character would be concerned about. Have students inhabit the character, consider their personal or professional stance, and think through these questions:

- What is the compelling story you want to tell or argument you want to make?
- What are you trying to persuade us about?
- What do you want (motivation)?
- What are the key themes or talking points you need to weave in to share your thinking?
- What is the emotional tone of what you're saying?

Visualization

Also referred to as guided imagery, visualization invites students to listen to a descriptive passage and imagine that they are experiencing the story as it unfolds. This strategy activates students' imaginations and can be used as a prewriting strategy or to help build background knowledge "both factual and emotional, about an event and to build interest on a topic or story" (DBI Network n.d., para. 1). The narrative can be written in second person (you). As students are listening, they can close their eyes (if comfortable doing so) to enhance the experience.

Drama across the Curriculum

Here are some simple drama activities that can be used at any grade level. All are easy to implement in any classroom; learning through drama does not require elaborate sets or intricate costumes.

Drama in Language Arts

Becoming a character in a story and exploring a situation through drama deepens comprehension skills and the ability to visualize what is happening and understand characters' choices. Have students create a voice collage in which they read aloud a series of carefully selected character voices from a book. The juxtaposing voices should overlap, bringing multiple voices into a space exploring themes of the text. Students can create tableaux based on critical moments from texts or write and perform short scenes as different characters.

In the Classroom

Middle school teachers in Maine devised an innovative approach using tableaux to explore a variety of moments in *The Phantom Tollbooth* by Norton Juster. The entire class used the drama strategy to create a life-size road map of Milo's trip. Not only did the living map retell Milo's trip; it showed the life lessons he learned along the way. At each place he stopped, the students created their tableaux of who or what was there and morphed their human sculpture into the lesson Milo learned. Cindy Denny, a teacher in Alaska, used the book *Cindy Ellen: A Wild Western Cinderella* by Susan Lowell (2000) to work on word choice from a six-trait writing rubric. She asked her students to imagine that Cindy Ellen and the other characters from the book were invited to appear on a talk show. Students took on the roles of different characters and were interviewed by the talk show host and the audience (the rest of the class). Students discussed how getting into the role of various characters brings out "voice" and enriches and deepens understanding. They identified how various characters' voices were different and led to word choices. Students then went on to create a dramatization of an alternate ending to the book. Students edited their endings, then exchanged with another group for editing, working toward a final draft. Students then acted out their alternate endings in their small groups.

Drama in Social Studies

Students often see history as being disconnected from their lives. Bring history to life by asking students to imagine they are a person from times past. Have them explore the idea of monologue by writing a journal entry for a historical figure or imaginary person living in the time they are studying. Or have small groups of students act out pivotal moments in history, then explore how the scenes would have been different if alternate decisions had been made by the characters.

Have groups of students create pantomime and act out (without speaking) the character traits of a historical figure, showing the traits through movement. As each small group shares their pantomime, exemplifying one trait, have the rest of the class describe what they see, generating a rich list of descriptions for the vocabulary being explored.

Once students have developed characters and explored a historical story through drama, you can "hot seat" a character by having students interview the character about their choices, beliefs, background, and so on. Students often are amazed at the knowledge that a character can share about their life and circumstances. This develops and reveals comprehension through perspective sharing in a deeply engaging way.

In the Classroom

Third grade teacher Denise Chesbro introduced students to the Norman Rockwell painting "Freedom of Speech," which depicts a community member speaking during a town meeting. After analyzing the painting for artistic choices, and how freedom is explored, students took on the poses of the subjects of the painting in a still tableau and discussed how they might feel if they had been there. Next, students acted out a "class meeting" to discuss important issues. The use of drama, both in taking on poses of subjects in the painting and in acting out a "class meeting" similar to a town meeting helped students deepen their understanding of what happens in local government, and why it is important (e.g., to give the citizens a say in their government).

Denise noted "Students were looking very critically at the original image to recreate it. They were having deep conversations about how they might represent the image, where in the room they should stage it, how they would create the different levels within the image, and who would 'play' each character. I was impressed with their willingness to try multiple [approaches]. They were able to feel . . . as if they were the character. Allowing students to take the driver's seat in their own learning is so empowering, and helps them to make connections and to utilize the arts to learn and express their own learning. . . . Students are empathetic. Empathy helps students understand historical events and the people who experienced them in first person. . . . When students can make a connection, they are much more likely to remember and understand."

Drama in Mathematics

Invite students to imagine they have been hired to create an advertisement that shows why the world needs geometry. Students should create a slogan, such as "Got Math?" and short informational segments on the use of geometric principles. This activity engages students in making sense of mathematical ideas, relating these ideas to real life, and using their own language and creativity to share the ideas. Students can then perform their series of commercials for other classes.

Have students dramatize word problems, inviting them to invent characters and situations to make the problems more engaging. Allow them to use crazy props and costume pieces to flesh out the scenarios. They can invite the audience to calculate at key moments in the drama.

Drama in Science

You can use drama to allow students to enact scientific ideas through simulation. Students can explore the relationship between organelles and cellular structure or act out scientific processes such as imagining a heart is a character reflecting on its role in the body through a monologue (Odegaard 2003). Or engage students in taking on the role of a scientist (Mantle of the Expert) and working through a scientific study. You might consider dramatizing moments of scientific discovery, such as the discovery of the X-ray, to consider how scientific thinking and processes yield results and build an awareness of how progress is made.

Ask students to take on the Mantle of the Expert on a scientific subject. Tell the "experts" that they need to review and interpret bar charts and graphs on the most current temperature statistics and draw inferences based on what the data say, then present their findings in a monologue.

In the Classroom

A kindergarten teacher asked her students to imagine they were scientists examining bones that she had created from paper maché. Based on the examination of bones through their observations and critical thinking, the junior scientists decided whether the bones belonged to a land dweller, sea dweller, or air dweller. The conversation held among the scientists revealed their scientific reasoning and understanding of the content.

Combining Drama with Other Art Forms

Have students use drama strategies to perform works in other art forms such as stories, poems, and music. Dramatize poetry by giving small groups different stanzas and asking the groups to act out the text. Students can bring their own interpretations to bear through inventive choices—the repetition of lines, addition of characters, pantomimed movement, choral voices, and solo voices. Use storytelling to introduce a dramatic activity by offering a context or situation that can then be explored more fully through the development of scenes. Have students incorporate music into drama to create a mood, represent a character, heighten awareness, or punctuate moments.

Concluding Thoughts

Drama integration allows students to connect with curricular content in ways that develop ownership and imagination. Students make their thinking visible as they become characters, improvise scenes, and embody stories. As students examine the role of stories in history, science, and literature, they can understand themselves better and, at the same time, develop the ability to value a multitude of perspectives. Using their imaginations and critical-thinking skills, students learn through active engagement, improve their communication skills, and develop their own sense of voice.

Drama also allows students to enjoy the process of learning. Teacher Kate DePalo describes what she notices happening as drama comes into her classroom: "They are internalizing conflicts, problem solving, and are becoming more involved in the material being taught. Most importantly, I have noticed that these drama strategies have brought the essence of play into my classroom. My students are not only learning, but they are having a blast doing it" (pers. comm.).

Through drama, we can give students the time and space to learn the lessons of life, exploring how one might react and respond to situations in particular contexts, and the unique chance to step outside of their personal frames of reference to understand how others think, feel, and react. A powerful connection between people and issues can be created in this space. Placing students as characters in fictional scenarios can provide them with opportunities for authentic responses that help them understand how people change and develop in response to their circumstances (O'Neill and Lambert 1991). Drama integration can help students of all ages locate their personal voices and ultimately their identities.

Reflection

1. Where in your curriculum would exploring different perspectives deepen learning or create empathy?

2. How might embodying a character allow students to experience a story or historical moment from the inside out?

3. Choose one drama strategy described in this chapter. How could you integrate this strategy into your existing curriculum?

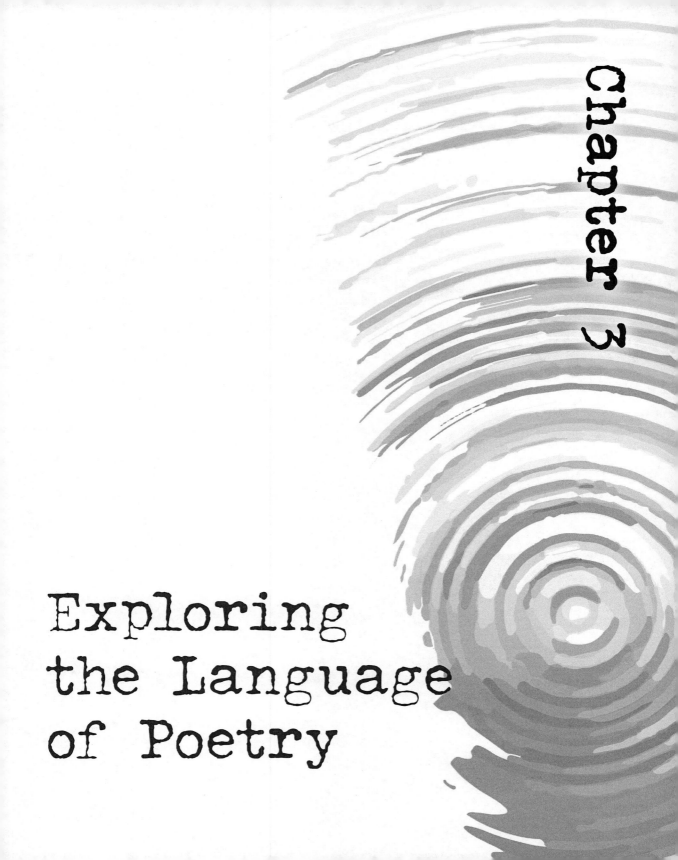

Chapter 3

Exploring
the Language
of Poetry

Exploring the Language of Poetry

What Is Poetry?

Amy Ludwig VanDerwater suggests, "Poems are the words of people who long to tell stories, teach, invite thoughts" (2018, XII).

Poetry is a unique use of language. Merryl Goldberg, in her book *Arts Integration*, suggests that poetry is "a playing with words" (2012). Poetry suggests rather than tells. It accentuates metaphor and image. Emily Dickinson captures the essence of poetry so beautifully in the first line of her poem "Tell all the Truth but tell it slant—" (Johnson 1960). That's what poetry allows us to do—to use language with a bit of freedom; to put words together without worrying about rules of grammar and punctuation. "Poetry is a language organized, produced, and experienced as an art form. If someone believes something is poetry, then, as far as I'm concerned, it is poetry" (Morice 1995).

Poetry provides us with a way to perceive the world, to see things in great detail and through all the senses. It's about paying attention, observing, being awake in the moment, and looking for sights, sounds, smells, feelings, and more. It's a way of playing with language, using image, repetition, pattern, sound, metaphor, and mood. When approached creatively, the result is a passion for writing and listening to poetry. Poetry can provide students a taste of freedom and pleasure with language.

Why Does Poetry Matter?

Richard Blanco, poet and Education Ambassador of the Academy of American Poets, has spoken directly to educators, saying, "I think of our nation's poets as citizen journalists, as activists, as heroes, and emotional historians. Indeed, they are the very storytellers of our democracy in progress. You give students the opportunity to hear those stories and to revel in the poetry of our nation" (2017).

Joy Harjo, first American Indian Poet Laureate and a member of the Muscogee (Creek) Nation, explains that "poetry is the voice of what can't be spoken, the mode of truth-telling when meaning needs to rise above or skim below everyday language in shapes not discernible by the ordinary mind. It trumps the rhetoric of politicians. Poetry is prophetic by nature and not bound by time. Because of these qualities poetry carries grief, heartache, ecstasy, celebration, despair, or searing truth more directly than any other literary art form. It is ceremonial in nature. Poetry is a tool for disruption and creation and is necessary for generations of humans to know who they are and who they are becoming in the wave map of history. Without poetry, we lose our way" (2019, para. 12). Harjo describes the unique ability of poetry to hold emotion and meaning and transcend every day language.

Including poetry as an integral part of education can engage students and help them bring together critical thinking and reflection. Listening to beautiful language filled with poetic images captures children's imaginations and deepens the intricacies of language such as metaphor, simile, and sound patterns created by alliteration. Poetry gives teachers authentic text in which to work on phonics, phonemic awareness, fluency, comprehension, writing, and language development skills such as rhyme, word families, and alliteration (Gill 2007; Perfect 1999; Whitin 1982). Rasinski explains that "poetry provides many opportunities for authentic oral practice. When students rehearse their reading of a poem, they repeatedly read the text aloud for a real purpose—to prepare to perform it expressively and meaningfully for an audience" (2014, 30).

Standards

Poetry in the College and Career Readiness Standards

Poetry is a genre that naturally and inherently addresses the standards in language arts. Describe, analyze, narrate, explain, listen, speak, and write using alliteration and metaphor—these are all skills found in the standards that are beautifully addressed through poetry. Reading, writing, and understanding poetry are an integral part of the standards for reading as well as speaking and listening. Poetry is listed as a type of literature students should read, and skills related to poetry are woven through the standards. For example, students are expected to understand figurative language, word relationships, and nuanced meanings (grade 8), analyze the impact of rhymes and other repetitions of sound (grade 7), and create audio recordings of poems that demonstrate fluid reading (grade 3). Writing poetry provides students an opportunity to apply what they have learned about language through their reading of poetry. Through poetry, teachers can address many standards related to phonics, phonemic awareness, language development, fluency, comprehension, word recognition, vocabulary development, use of metaphor and simile, and imagery.

Poems provide a simpler context for students to practice these skills, using text that is at their interest and academic level (Stickling, Prasun, and Olsen 2011). Writing poetry temporarily frees students from some of the conventions of writing, which they often find restrictive, and allows them to focus on theme, word choice, and the music of language.

Poetry is a powerful tool to expand content learning beyond the language arts as well. In social studies, reading poetry can bring students to the heart and soul of the culture or era they are studying. The rhythm and pattern in poetry are certainly mathematical. And creating poetry about science and mathematics helps students create mental images and forge new understanding.

Through reading and writing poetry, students are free to take risks and express their deep feelings that precede critical analysis.

Mary Oliver notes, "Poetry is a life-cherishing force. And it requires a vision—a faith, to use an old-fashioned term. Yes, indeed. For poems are not words, after all, but fires for the cold, ropes let down to the lost, something as necessary as bread in the pockets of the hungry. Yes, indeed" (1994).

Poet Naomi Shihab Nye explains, "Sometimes one of the most precious elements of affinity and inspiration is gathering up poems so that you'll be able to put your fingers on them later to hand to someone at the appropriate moment, to give to the friend who needs it right then, to email to the person who's hurting" (2011).

A high school English teacher in California used poetry with a group of students who struggled with success when taught with traditional educational approaches. She sensed that perhaps using this strategy might interest them. She began by first reading her own *I Am From* poem (see page 80 for more information). Aware of her students' difficult life situations, she explained that it was not necessary to share every detail of their lives, and she had carefully decided what to put in her own poem and what details to leave out. She gave her students some topics to explore, such as home, memories, neighborhood, particular sayings they remember, or special places. She encouraged them to bring in details—sights, sounds, smells, and so on.

> "For poems are not words, after all, but fires for the cold, ropes let down to the lost, something as necessary as bread in the pockets of the hungry."
>
> —Mary Oliver (1994)

Once the class began working on the assignment, the teacher became aware that one student, who had struggled all year and spent most of his time unengaged and uninterested, was writing with fervor. When he finished, he approached her with excitement and asked if he could go to the computer lab to type his poem. It was the first time the teacher had seen him write with such substance. He returned and proudly turned in an extraordinary poem. The following is an excerpt from his poem:

> I am from the city of God, the land of lords, the foothill of
> life, the lights of the moon and stars. I am from the city
> of racism. I am from the land of freedom.
>
> I am from the piss in the hallway. I am from the streets,
> the cold hard streets.
>
> I am from the land where people die on corners. I am
> from the land that everybody wants to live in but where I
> will die in.
>
> I am from the city where you have to watch your back.
> I am from the land that never dies. I am from a place
> where they told me I would never make it; never finish. I
> am from the ghetto and I will make it!
>
> —High school student, California (2007)

For this particular student, and for many students, writing a poem touches something deep inside. Poetry gave this student a vehicle for expression, voicing the intense frustration and pent-up emotions that hitherto he had left unsaid. His voice, up until that moment, was rarely heard. This poetry exercise opened a door that had previously been closed.

We know that relationship, being known, and being seen for who we are—our hopes, our fears, and our experiences—is foundational to student learning. This student expressed his heart when he wrote, "I am from a place where they told me I would never make it; never finish." Through the vehicle of poetry, the relationships among students, peers, and teachers encourage and strengthen a classroom community of support. Poetry, like the other art forms, not only gives students a powerful voice but allows them to be successful in ways that might not be possible through conventional educational strategies. Because of poetry, this student's teacher was able to connect with him and support him in his learning.

Bring Poetry into Your Life

Many of us read news articles and social media posts online, peruse magazines, enjoy novels, and dive into nonfiction works with gusto. But how many of us read poetry on a regular basis? Probably not many. Why not? What has stopped us? Is it too hard? Too complicated? Not accessible? Too much work to figure out? Perhaps poetry holds unpleasant memories from school when we were required to dissect a poem with such doggedness that it lost all meaning. Now, any enjoyment the reading of poetry held for us in the past has disappeared. Poet Georgia Heard says, "For many of us poetry has seemed like a door, locked tight with a chain and a heavy padlock across it" (1999, 43).

"Reading, writing and performing poetry engages students to work through familial, communal, social, and emotional issues. Reading original poetry aloud in class can foster trust and empathy in the classroom community, while also emphasizing speaking and listening skills."

—Jessica Helen Lopez (2018, para. 5)

On the other hand, there are probably large numbers of us who have pleasant memories of chanting jump rope rhymes, nursery rhymes, table graces, nighttime prayers, and several other poetic pieces that we can still happily rattle off today, years later. These poetic verses were fun to learn and continue to be a joy to recite. What is the difference? Perhaps it is the love of poetry, the sheer pleasure in the sounds, rhythms, words, and images.

Many teachers avoid poetry, dread teaching it, do not think of themselves as poets, and thus miss the opportunity to use it as an essential teaching strategy. Kenneth Koch (1999), author of the magical book of children's poetry *Wishes, Lies and Dreams: Teaching Children to Write Poetry*, has taught poetry in New York public schools for years and feels that children are not given the exposure to valuable writing, because teachers are intimidated by it and have the false impression that children are unable to respond to poetry—that it is "too difficult" or too stylized for children to comprehend, never mind comment on. In fact, Koch's examples of children's poetic writing affirm their ability to grasp complicated concepts as well as relate such complexities to their own emotions (Poetry Foundation n.d.). Teachers, too, can be renewed by poetry and can see that it speaks to their needs, to their yearnings, to their deepest experiences. One of Koch's students sums up why poetry is important: "I like poetry because it puts me in places I like to be" (Koch 2012).

"Can you see yourself or society in this poem? How does the poem encourage us to do something—to hope; grieve; celebrate; remember?"

—Jenn Bogard, Author of *The ABCs of Plum Island, Massachusetts* (a mentor text for found poetry using primary sources)

Before introducing poetry in your classroom, bring poetry back into your own life. Visit the library and sit in front of the stacks of poetry books. Pull some off the shelf and scan them. What interests you? Which poems do you enjoy? Are there poetry books that remind you of topics you teach? Ask your community librarian to help you curate a collection of poetry books to take home and peruse. You might subscribe to a poem-a-day through the Academy of American Poets or the Poetry Foundation.

Once you feel comfortable and confident reading and writing poetry, your enthusiasm and experience will transfer to the students, and the students, too, will find similar joy. Step one is to overcome any preconceptions long held about what poetry really is or what it means to write poetry or be a poet.

Read Poetry

Begin by reading and enjoying poetry yourself. See what touches you. Find poems that you like, that please you. You'll soon discover that there are poets with whom you resonate, who seem to describe experiences like you might have had. If there are poems you like, bring them to class and read them to students. Although there are times for analyzing poetry, there should also be many opportunities to just soak in the words without analysis. Poetry can be a presence in a classroom, without any interpretation, without any commentary. Simply make a place for poetry. Enjoy the process.

Write Poetry

Next, draft a poem. Start by choosing one of these ideas to spark your process:

1. Draw a map of the place where you grew up. Put everything on it—the local school or place of worship, your tree house, the park where you hung out, the hill you sledded down. Use this map to connect to your memories. Pick one vivid memory and do a mind map, listing everything you can about that memory. Work through your senses. What sights, sounds, tastes, or smells do you remember? List the details. Who was there? What did it feel like? What was the weather like? What were you wearing? What textures do you remember? What time of day was it? Take the details of this one memory and put it into a loose poetic form. Create a list poem. This could be a list of dishes you cook; things that make you happy, confused, sad; questions you have; names of dogs you've loved; and more.

2. Think of an object that is meaningful to you and draft a few words about it. Don't worry about getting it "right."

Here are a few guidelines to follow as a way to get started:

- **Play with the rhythm and beat.** Were you taught that poems have to rhyme? Free yourself of the idea that all poems use end rhyme, and enjoy creating a rhythm and beat in your own unique way. Consider playing with different patterns and arrangements of syllables or repeating a phrase, word, or line. Read your poem aloud, and listen to the sounds of the words and syllables.

- **Write in phrases rather than full sentences.** You are creating impressions, details, and suggestions of meaning. This is part of the joy of breaking out of standard English syntax and diction. Write in fragments or phrases. You might try setting a word on a line of its own for impact.

- **Show, don't tell.** Use sensory words. Give an impression of what happened. Bring it to life through emotions and all the senses. Resist telling the reader what to think or how to interpret what you are saying. There is no need to point to the obvious. Play around. The heart of a poem lies in its images—word pictures that the poet paints to re-create a scene, an experience, a memory, and so on. Images are drawn from the senses—seeing, hearing, smelling, tasting, touching. Poetry is grounded in the tangible world. Using images enables your poetry to *show* what you are writing about rather than *telling* or summarizing it.

- **Move beyond clichés.** Poetry does not require fancy words. The words you use to speak with are strong and will be equally strong when you write them down. There is no one to impress. Don't worry about coming up with "poetic words." Choose every word because it is the best, freshest, least clichéd word you can think of. Focus on precise word choices to communicate meaning.

- **Use metaphor to compare two things.** Writing using metaphor is an attempt to condense language and vividly connect two unlike things together, such as *My words are kites.* Metaphor can heighten understanding and invite us to see things in fresh ways. For example, in Carl Sandburg's poem "Fog," the inanimate fog is compared to a living cat to bring the fog to life. A metaphor (or simile, using *like* or *as*) helps your poetry "leap," that is, to move from one category of thought to another, to easily and powerfully summarize how one thing resembles another, and thus illuminate the first idea with an economy of words. Metaphors are powerful, and metaphorical thinking is a higher-order thinking skill; it takes practice.

- **Read your poem aloud to yourself to hear its rhythm.** Rhythm exists naturally in language, and most of us are delighted by it. Line breaks can help create a rhythm that supports the meaning of the words you are writing and fosters complex and pleasant thought.

Once you have something on paper, go back and revisit it again and again. Work with it. Revise it. Put it away and get it out again . . . and again. If you can, read it to someone else, and have that person help you revise it.

And finally, share it. Some poems are meant to be read aloud; you can honor a poem by giving it an audience. Or you can give it away. In this way, you complete the writer/reader connection that happens in all art forms, the sharing of the created piece. Poems make delicious gifts.

Introduce Poetry to Students

Once you have experienced the power of poetry for yourself, you will be excited to share it with students. Georgia Heard advises us to "choose poems that are immediately accessible, nonthreatening, and relevant to students' lives" and to "encourage reading projects that will invite all students into the world of poetry" (1999, 21).

Begin by reading poetry to students and having them read it to each other. U.S. Poet Laureate Billy Collins argues that reading poetry develops some fundamental cognitive and intellectual skills, and that reading a poem "replicates the way we learn and think" (Showalter 2012, 63). He sees many parallels between poetry and learning: "When we read a poem, we enter the consciousness of another. It requires that we loosen some of our fixed notions in order to accommodate another point of view. . . . To follow the connections in a metaphor is to make a mental leap, to exercise an imaginative agility, even to open a new synapse as two disparate things are linked." Collins considers poetic form as "a way of thinking, an angle of approach" that helps students understand how information must be "shaped and contoured in order to be intelligible."

The best way to introduce poetry to students is to have them listen to poetry—all sorts of genres of poetry. Today's students are used to listening to all types of music, and they have quite a discerning ear. By listening to poetry, they begin to analyze language and appreciate how meaning is shaped. Listening to a variety of poems also allows them to consider ways in which identity may be perceived and understood as manifested in the poems they hear (Gordon 2009). Ask students what they remember about the poem they just heard. They are hearing meaning in their own way, through their own ears. What details do they remember? What stuck? Listening to and experiencing poems in sound are important dimensions of engaging with and understanding the meaning potential of texts and the means with which students readily involve themselves.

Our schools are filled with diverse learners, and it is important to read a diverse selection of poetry. A group of researchers in Canada discovered that poetry was the best practice not only for teaching literacy but for helping students develop critical-thinking and analytical perspectives, and the power of high-interest cultural content motivated language learners beyond all else (Reeves 2009).

Ideally, students should read and hear as many poems as possible so they can find their own style of poetry. They should hear traditional poetry as well as contemporary poetry and experience serious and humorous poetry. From this wide variety of poets and poems, students can connect with one or more genres and then move to writing their own poems (Lynch 2009).

As students hear more and more poetry, they will enjoy it more and more. Assumptions about what poetry is and is not will break down. Just as there is not one genre of music, there is not one genre of poetry. Listening to poems read aloud gives students a chance to feel, think, discover, ask questions, and, perhaps, get answers. You could begin by simply reading the title and asking students what they think the poem will be about. Ask them to listen to the sounds of the words. Once readers or listeners practice making sense of poetry, they may generalize this useful skill to other texts and genres (Stickling, Prasun, and Olsen 2011).

"Reading and analyzing poetry helps students have culturally responsive discussions because there's usually no single correct answer to a poem's meaning—since students will have many different points of view about an issue, poetry can give rise to riveting discussions."

—Jill Fletcher (2018, para. 11)

Help Students Discover Their Preferred Styles of Writing Poetry

While exposing students to all sorts of different poem types, guide them to notice that rhyming at the ends of lines is only one way to craft a poem. Some poems rhyme. Some poems do not rhyme. Ask students, "What do you prefer? Why?" For students who have a preconceived idea that poems have to rhyme, offer them the opportunity to write two poems about the same subject—one that rhymes at the end of lines and one that does not. They might discover that writing poetry provides much more freedom if they are not saddled with trying to find a rhyming word. Kwame Alexander explains, "Children love to rhyme, and many children's first books are rhymed books. Rhyming is fun. Words are fun. Let's also remember that young children already experience the world the way a poet does. Have you ever taken a toddler by the hand and tried to walk a few blocks? They notice everything—the sound of every passing car or insect, a coin shining on the sidewalk" (Alexander 2019, 28).

Figure 3.1 provides some suggested first poems to read aloud to students. Some of these poems have specific forms that students can use to model their own writing. It is a good place to help students begin developing their own poetic vocabulary. Musical lyrics also can be analyzed. Bob Dylan's lyrics are often used because of the ingenious way he stresses syllables and plays with metaphor. Figure 3.2 suggests poetry collections for classroom use. See Appendix D: Recommended Resources for more information.

Georgia Heard explains, "When I read a poem I first let it affect my heart. My curiosity about the poem begins with amazement and love. And my eagerness to search deeper into analyzing a poem's craft comes from my yearning as a poet to know my craft better, so I can better express my heart" (1999, 43).

Figure 3.1 Poems to Read Aloud

"The Aliens Have Landed" Jack Prelutsky	"Knoxville, Tennessee" Nikki Giovanni
"The Bronze Legacy" Effie Lee Newsome	"Not in Vain" Emily Dickinson
"Dreams" Langston Hughes	"Oranges" Gary Soto
"Don't Go into the Library" Alberto Rios	"Remember" Joy Harjo
"I Ask My Mother to Sing" Li-Young Lee	"Scaffolding" Seamus Heaney
"If—" Rudyard Kipling	"This Is Not a Small Voice" Sonia Sanchez
"If I Were in Charge of the World" Judith Viorst	"The Undefeated" Kwame Alexander

Visit these websites to find a wide range of poems from a variety of voices:

- National Council of Teachers of English Award for Excellence in Poetry for Children and Notable Poetry Books List, **ncte.org**
- Young People's Poet Laureates, **www.poetryfoundation.org/learn/young-peoples-poet-laureate**
- Poetry Foundation, **www.poetryfoundation.org**, for Ruth Lilly Poetry Prize winners
- Poems Kids Like, **poets.org/text/poems-kids**

Figure 3.2 Poetry Collections

Shel Silverstein	*Where the Sidewalk Ends* (1974) *A Light in the Attic* (1981) *Falling Up* (1996)
Jack Prelutsky	*New Kid on the Block* (1984) *Pizza the Size of the Sun* (1996) *Raining Pigs and Noodles* (2005)
Betsy Franco	*Messing Around on the Monkey Bars* (2009)
Alan Katz	*Oops* (2008)
Carol Diggory Shields	*Almost Late to School* (2003)
Sharon Creech	*Hate That Cat* (2008)

Once students are comfortable and enjoying listening to and reading poetry, invite them to create their own poems. The following activities will provide enough inspiration to get students started and allow for the creativity and expression that make poetry a rich teaching and learning tool.

Introductory Activity: Poetry about Change

Many curriculum areas include the concept of change. There are seasonal changes, climate changes, historical changes, changing states of matter, and psychological and physical changes, to name a few. All of these can be transformed into poetic verse! Here is a suggested lesson idea about change, inspired by a personal memory, to use as an introduction to the poetic process.

1. **Warm up:** Start by discussing with students what it means for something or someone to change. Brainstorm a list of things that change. The change can be big or small, something that happened quickly or something that took a long time (for example, changing homes, changing age, changing friendships, changing hairstyles, changing from riding a tricycle to a two-wheeler, changing an emotion, changing your mind, the change of seasons).

2. **Begin with a memory:** Ask students to try to remember something that changed in their own lives or a change from a shared class experience. Ask them to visualize where they were when the change happened: "What did it feel like? Who was there? What were you wearing? What season was it?"

3. **Create a visual picture of the "change memory":** With a range of art materials, have students create a picture of the memory—the place and the happening. The picture does not need to be perfect. It is simply a way to capture the memory visually and bring it to life.

4. **Jot words and phrases:** Have students write phrases about the change. They should avoid writing complete sentences; rather, they should bring the change to life through emotions and all the senses. They are trying to *show* the change through images rather than tell about it.

5. **Use metaphor or simile to compare things:** Show students how they can bring the change event to life by showing how one thing resembles another. As a class, brainstorm pairs of words and discuss how they relate to one another. This is a higher-order thinking skill and will be more difficult for younger children, but give it a try! See what happens. Have examples of metaphor and simile ready to share with the class.

6. **Share the poems:** Have students first read their poems to themselves. Encourage them to pay attention to the sound of the poem. Have them ask themselves the following: "Is there anything I want to change? Would other words provide a different rhythm? Can I make it more interesting? Have I read the poem aloud and shared it with another student?"

Poetry about Change: Curriculum Connections

Once students have created personal change poems, they can create change poems in any content area. Here are some ideas:

- **Social studies:** Choose a theme from your social studies unit. As a class, think about one aspect of that topic where change has occurred, and write a poem about it. For instance, students could write poems about how the adoption of the Constitution changed the United States or changes that have occurred in technology over the twentieth and twenty-first centuries.

- **Mathematics:** Numbers change: They increase and decrease; they can be added, divided, and multiplied; they become fractions. Have students write about a mathematical change from the viewpoint of a number.
- **Science:** Have students write about environmental change, perhaps a change from liquid to solid or the change of seasons. In addition to describing the change, they should describe their feelings and attitudes about it. Remind them to be specific and use all their senses in the description.

Poetry across the Curriculum

Here are some poetry activities that can be used at any grade level. Have students create personal poems first so they get the feel for each type of poem, then expand into the content areas.

Word Bowl

A good beginning poetry exercise is called "the word bowl." It gives you a leg up when facing the blank page and puts participants at ease. It allows for experimentation with words and images. Start by creating a list of words centered on a particular topic. Have students brainstorm, building a relevant list that includes pronouns, verbs, nouns, prepositional phrases, and so on. Find lively words, words that are humorous, attention-grabbing, or mesmerizing. Once you have a good, long list, write the words on paper and then cut them apart and put them in a large "word bowl."

Have student volunteers reach in and choose five or ten words from the bowl. Make up a poem together using these words, thinking about the theme or topic you chose. Have students try writing their own poems using these words. Read the poems aloud so students can see how many poems can come from the same words. Students will quickly get the idea and be eager to create their own. Word bowls are a great way for students to expand and work with vocabulary in any content area. This strategy also works well with nonfiction texts, allowing students to summarize and engage with dense material by drawing out relevant ideas and putting words and phrases together in interesting ways.

You also might have students cut their own words from magazines to add to their word bowls.

Sample of Word Bowl Poems

by Heidi Hopwood, Idaho

"I Am From" Poem

"I Am From" poems, developed by George Ella Lyon (2010), allow space for students to share about family traditions, home life, special moments, and memories. In this form, each line begins with the words *I am from*, and the poet then relates not only the places but the emotions, feelings, sights, sounds, smells, and tastes of their life. A wonderful resource and good introduction to this poetic form is *Mama, Where Are You From?* by Marie Bradby (2000).

"I Am From" poems invite the stories and voices of students into the classroom. "As we create schools and classrooms that are laboratories for a more just society than the one we now live in, we need to remember to make our students feel significant and cared about" (Christensen 2001).

Try writing your own "I Am From" poem first. Going through the process of creating an "I Am From" poem and then reading it to students is an excellent place to begin. It will give students insight into your life and provide them with a relevant example. You also will be able to talk about your process of writing the poem. Then, have students create their own "I Am From" poems based on their own lives. Here is an excerpt from an "I Am From" poem written by a teacher in Idaho:

> I am from an old wringer washer,
> A clothesline full of clothes; crunchy towels, stiff jeans
> And sheets that smell like sunshine.
> I am from homemade bread, hot cereal for breakfast,
> pea soup
> And white, pasty, lima beans.
> I am from canning eternal boxes of fruit and garden
> produce in the summer.
>
> —Liz Thurgood, Educator,
> Coeur d'Alene, Idaho

The "I Am From" poem carries quite easily into any content area. Have students write "I Am From" poems from the point of view of historical figures (social studies), literary characters (language arts), animals (biology), rocks (geology), planets (astronomy), or even geometric solids or graphs (mathematics).

Darwin

> I am from science
> Looking farther into nature
> Studying the life I see
> Flourishing everywhere
> The similarities between different animals
> And differences between the same
> I notice things overlooked by religion and
> Study them in secret
> The things we have discovered will change so much.
>
> —Elliot Winston,
> sixth-grade student

Observation Poem

Invite students to use all their senses to experience something—a place, time, or object. Have them note the sizes, shapes, colors, and textures they see, feel, and hear. Ask them to describe the smells and tastes they experience. Then have them create poems based on these sensory images.

> *The pot looks like a pear with a mouth.*
> *The pot's color looks sometimes like the sky*
> *With wind around it.*
> *The pot smells like clay with vanilla mixed.*
> *It feels like a rough rock with a hole.*
> *It is hollow like a cave.*
> *I can fit a genie in it.*

—Fifth-grade student
(McKim and Steinbergh 2004, 59)

Observation poems are a great extension to students' recordings of scientific observation. Have them write poems about their experiences observing nature or performing experiments. Just be careful with taste and smell in the lab.

Ode

An ode celebrates and praises. Traditionally an ode exalts the qualities of its subject, illustrating it with elevated praise, but modern poets have come to use odes to describe everyday things.

For the classroom, we teach the premise of an ode—to honor, celebrate, and praise—and encourage students to be creative in how they would like to structure their poem. We find this inspires a love for poetry.

A Greek god named Poseidon
A brother to Zeus and Hades
He was a god who ruled the sea.
Quick tempered. . . like the Hulk!!!
A provoker of earthquakes,
His anger caused big tsunamis.
In my opinion he's the best of all
With his trident he was like . . .
Aquaman!!!
Like the Flash . . .
with superspeed!!!
He rides in a chariot
drawn by four horses
over the sea.

—Sean Delaney, Jr.
Hudson Junior High School

What some words mean:
Quick tempered: gets angry quickly
A provoker of earthquakes: makes earthquakes

Poems Inspired by Memories

We all have poignant memories about moments that affected us deeply. Inviting students to write about a memory can yield rich details of time and place. Before writing, ask students questions to help them sketch or jot notes about the memory: "About how old were you? Who was with you? What emotions did you experience?" Have students describe their memories through the lens of their five senses. These descriptions can serve as jumping-off points for students to capture this moment in time through poetry.

Sewing Contentment

*Mom guiding the fabric through
the foot smoothly/pausing to snip loose
threads/the majestic Singer rhythmically edges
its way along the seam/the mesmerizing
motion of the treadle/the little girl trailing behind
fixated on the lace trim, feeling the softness in
its curves/the slight rigidness keeping its
shape in daily life/the eyelet providing a new
lens to look through/growing into a more
modern model/moving faster now/creating
movement and swing from the tissue
patterns/style with grace/maxi to mini and
beehive to bob/peace signs with flower petals
to shimmering pools of silver/turning out suits
with vests fashioning the growing girl/the
smoothness of the buttons, delicate yet sturdy,
hand sewn, an anchor for the button yet a hole
to slip through/to the store bought skirt with the kick
pleat/to hemming a pant leg or a summer
dress/to the new tablecloth and new curtains
made for the new me/to the slowing down—
the unwinding of the spool, a sock to darn, a button
put back on/the limp garment on the back of
the chair/to the quietness of the gathering
dust/to waiting to be alive again/to have the
fabric guided into the path of the needle/to
recreate the magic and have an even straight
path again...if just for a moment.*

—MaryAnn Murphy
Educator and Poet
Hudson City School District *(retired)*

Still Life with Memory

Forsythia skeletons set spindly shadows on stone walls
A sun-bleached wooden plough is covered with vines, and sticks
Near an abandoned wheelbarrow leaning against the dark opening.
Pebbles and leaves cover the cold earth in front of the shed.
All is still.
It smelled musty inside,
The dirt floor felt cold against my feet.
The wine barrels, rusty nails, bottles caps,
Fallen branches, and broken glass
Made a gray and dusty nest for the old iron stove.
Her gardening tools, a pitchfork and a hoe stood silent in the doorway.
The weeds, the yellow grass, the dried leaves and
Barren spots of dirt surrounding the shed
Became a fragrant garden under my eight-year-old, bare feet.
She bent forward and picked juicy tomatoes and spicy peppers,
Filling the pockets of her floral apron.
The soil was warm and rich, and the shed looked golden in the sunlight.
And I remember eating freshly tossed salad upstairs from the shed
In my grandmother's sweet-smelling kitchen.

—Alicia Chiasson

Persona Poem

Poems from a specific entity's point of view, or *persona poems*, extend the imagination and allow for freedom of voice. In this type of poetry, the writer "becomes" an object or concept and writes about their experience. There are objects everywhere, and each holds the potential of becoming the inspiration for a poem—a falling leaf, burning candle, archaeological artifact, historical document, fractal, number, mathematical equation. The excitement for students is to make the connection with their object or concept, get to know it, identify with it, and become the object. They should ask themselves questions such as "How do I feel? What do I like best about myself? How do I move? Do I have a special sound or language or smell or taste? Where did I come from? What is my daily life like? What do I believe? How does it feel to be changed into something else?"

Here are examples of two persona poems written by fifth graders from Coeur d'Alene, Idaho, as part of their study of plant and animal cells.

I Am a Red Blood Cell

My extravagant red color is ordinary
In this quiet, slippery tube
My nucleus is commanding
"Mitochondria, more ENERGY!"
Because all my parts have important jobs
Sometimes it's tedious
Just flowing and listening
To the only sound anyone can hear.
Breathing
Everyone here is individual
But we are all smooth and round
Which helps us flow effortlessly through this vein
Our animal owner needs us red blood cells
Without us he would die
Then we would have no job
So we would die too
I am a red blood cell

—Fifth-grade student, Idaho

The Life of a Nerve Cell

I am a nerve cell.
Wait!
I have a message!
Good thing I am a branching shape.
Wait! Message!
I sent this message already!
I am glad
That I have a good nucleus
Or else I would go crazy!
Wait! Message!
It is already hot in here
And all this work makes it hotter.
My shape helps because the message can scurry up me.
Like a squirrel up a tree.
Here is another message!
Bye!

—Fifth-grade student, Idaho

Age Poem

Have students begin a poem with either "I am in the beginning of my _____ year" or an introductory line that refers to their age. Then have them write about their life at that point. Tell them to think about games they played, names of friends and teachers, school events, family events, summer pastimes, favorite clothes and foods, and so on. This is similar to "I Am From" poems but not as commonly done. Age poems prompt students to look at things from a new perspective. Students can create age poems for historical figures, literary characters, or even scientific principles.

Fourteen Year Oxymoron

To be fourteen is to be old and young at the same
time. It is a time of clear confusion and happy
sadness. It is a dream in reality. Oh! This age! Sane
craziness, right wrongness, pleasurable pain. How
short and long it is. When I am older, I know I will
think those were the awfully good times.

(Lown and Steinbergh 1996)

Forms of Poetry

Some poets enjoy the freedom of free-verse poems, and others appreciate having a structure to guide them. When asking students to write poetry, offer them many choices, including a frame in which to safely create. Here are a few suggestions of forms of poetry to explore.

Acrostic

Acrostic poems are written around a topic word. The topic word is written vertically, and each letter begins a line related to the topic.

Ladybugs eat aphids
A ladybug is pretty
Disgusting smells come out when they are scared
Yellow when they come from pupa
Beetles are bugs
Up in the sky flying high
Gardens are where you find them

(Frye, Trathen, and Schlagal 2010)

Cinquain

Cinquain poetry has five lines:

Line 1: two syllables

Line 2: four syllables

Line 3: six syllables

Line 4: eight syllables

Line 5: two syllables

Hide and Seek

You're it!
I'm hiding fast
behind the big oak tree
I'm in a tent of young green leaves
Got you!

—Mary Clare Powell

Plants

I am
a plant, I grow
from a tiny brown seed
I need air, water and sunlight
Flower!

—Mary Clare Powell

Diamante

Diamante poems, or diamond-shaped poems, start with one word on the first line, grow to four words, then go back to one word. The basic structure is:

Line 1: one word—subject/noun that is contrasting to line 7

Line 2: two words—adjectives that describe line 1

Line 3: three words—verbs that relate to line 1

Line 4: four words—nouns: first two words relate to line 1, last two words to line 7

Line 5: three words—action verbs that relate to line 7

Line 6: two words—adjectives that describe line 7

Line 7: one word—subject/noun that is contrasting to line 1

A diamante poem can describe one concept:

Arctic

Arctic
Blustery, desolate
Swirling, screaming, freezing
Caribou, igloos . . . Camels, tents
Burning, blinding, whistling
Barren, dry
Desert

—Vincent, age 13, Indiana (2008)

A diamante poem can move from one vocabulary word to its antonym:

Morning

Morning
bright, no clouds
stretch, jump up, eat
school and work, play and supper
slow down, rest, relax
cool, dark
evening

—Mary Clare Powell

Or a diamante poem can describe a process:

Caterpillar

Caterpillar
Fuzzy, small
Inching, eating, fattening,
Small, green—colorful, graceful
Cocooning, growing, dreaming
Bright, in flight
Butterfly

—Taffy Lovell (2008)

List

List poetry is one of the most accessible forms to write. It is made up of a list of items or events and can be any length, rhymed or unrhymed. The topic of a list poem can range from "waiting" to "what bugs me" to any curriculum subject matter. For instance, to reinforce understanding of verbs and prepositions, a list poem could be created in which every line uses a verb or preposition. Any topic can work!

Fall

*Sweet smell
Of autumn leaves
Clusters of color on the forest floor
Red
Orange
Yellow
Cool breeze
Snuggling in my sweater
Cold nose
Warm breath
Collecting apples in a basket
C r u n c h
Explosion of sweet juice
Running down my chin*

Concrete

Concrete poems are written so that the placement of the text forms the shape of the subject of the poem. A poem about a triangle would be shaped like a triangle, and a poem about a tree would be shaped like a tree.

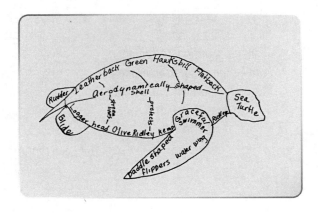

Haiku

Haiku poetry comes from Japan. Haiku poems have three lines. The first line has five syllables, the second line has seven syllables, and the third line has five syllables. Haiku poems do not rhyme, and often the topic is related to nature or the seasons.

Haiku Seasonal Cycle

*The lilies open
To announce a new season
Snow rabbits change hue.*

*The fox finds freedom
Heat waves rise off the moths' wings
The goldfish all swim.*

*Sharp, crisp winds blowing
Frost forms on the spider web
The animals hide.*

*The world is white now
Flaky snow from flaky clouds
Look forward to spring.*

—Fifth-grade student
(as cited in McKim and Steinbergh 2004, 129)

Sharing Poetry

Sometimes we write poems just for ourselves. We might want to explore our thoughts or save memories. But other poems are for sharing. Here are a few ways for students to share their poems:

- **Chapbooks:** A chapbook is a pocket-size book meant for carrying. Collect students' original poems and put them together in a little book. Publish multiple copies to share with parents and other classes.
- **Poetry cards:** Have students create original poetry greeting cards for special occasions. They can give them to family and friends.
- **Publishing station:** Set up an area in the classroom for students to publish their poetry. Include small booklets, paper, pencils and pens, crayons and markers, decorative stamps, staplers, and tape—whatever students might need to publish their works.
- **Readings:** The music of poetry is best experienced when it is read aloud. Invite parents, administrators, and other classes to a poetry reading where students read their original works aloud to thunderous applause!
- **Hidden poems:** Invite students to hide poems around the classroom or at home for others to find.

Concluding Thoughts

Paul Janeczko confesses in *Reading Poetry in the Middle Grades* that he wishes the culture today was one in which he didn't have to work so hard to convince others that poetry counts (2011). In education today, poetry is often neglected or considered a frill.

There is a wonderfully inspiring book, *Teaching with Fire: Poetry That Sustains the Courage to Teach* (Intrator and Scribner 2003), that contains not only powerful poetry but an introduction to each poem written by a teacher wherein she explains how one particular poem has sustained or helped her reach her students in new ways. Poetry has the power to do that. It can bring meaning not only to our students but to ourselves as well. "Poetry often gets a bad rap as stodgy and highfalutin. Poet Laureate Billy Collins reminds us to lighten up, and let poetry reach us in things that are human and real" (Intrator and Scribner 2003, 194).

After reading this chapter on exploring the language of poetry, hopefully you can see that poetry has great value for you and students. In 2002, a group of students who participated in a 15-week "Poet in Residence" program, which involved both writing and reading poetry, demonstrated significant achievement in expressive writing, increased vocabulary, and improved critical-analysis skills and reading comprehension. And more important, during interviews with the students and focus groups following the residency, there was clear indication of an increased positive attitude about writing. Students who were struggling with writing and reading showed marked improvement (Slater 2002).

When students attempt to make sense of a poem, they use critical-analysis skills to understand and make meaning. They become sensitive to the mood and sounds of words. When they write their own poetry, these skills transfer. Through their own creativity, they are able to express their thoughts and feelings. Their voices are heard. Sharing our own voices and listening to others is a gift that must be a part of everyone's educational experience. We owe it to students and ourselves.

Reflection

1. What is your "poetry attitude" that has been influenced by past poetry experiences?

2. How comfortable are you with using poetry in the classroom?

3. Choose one lesson you plan to teach in the next week. How can you integrate poetry? What content–area objectives could you address using poetry? What form of poetry would you use? How would you assess the content learned through poetry?

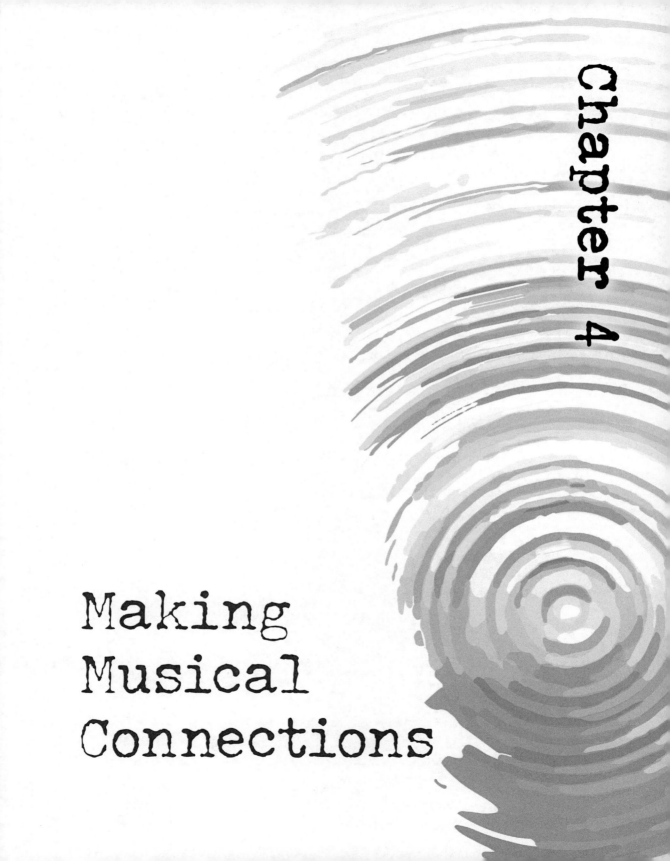

Chapter 4

Making
Musical
Connections

Making Musical Connections

What Is Music?

The basic elements of music, primarily from a Western framework, include rhythm/tempo, harmony, dynamics, melody, timbre, texture, and pitch. Some or all of these elements are an integral part of most musical compositions, whether instrumental or vocal. But is it possible to have a musical piece that has no clear tone? No melody or pitch? Yes, it is. So what, then, could be the most basic definition of *music* and one that encompasses all music, from all cultures and all genres? Can rattling some pots and pans be music? Does tapping a pencil gently on a desk become a musical composition? The answer, we believe, is yes. How can that be possible? What is the distinction between noise and music?

Music is intentional or organized sound (and silence), often using elements such as rhythm, melody, harmony, pitch, and more. If someone bangs randomly on a pile of pots and pans, it makes noise. If the person bangs on them in a rhythmic way, they are making music. *Stomp Out Loud*, a unique musical theater production featuring choreographed percussion and movement, has revolutionized the idea of what it is to make music. The *Stomp* performers use ordinary objects such as chairs and trash cans, which most of us would never consider "playing" as musical instruments, to create wonderfully engaging compositions. Now that we can consider brooms or keys to be musical instruments, the possibilities are endless. (A link to the *Stomp* video can be found in the Music Resources section in Appendix D.)

For those of us who are not familiar with musical terms and/or do not "read" musical notation, a complicated definition that uses a term such as *timbre* can be off-putting. Is it possible to integrate music in a classroom when you can't read music and have no idea what the word *timbre* means? Thinking in terms of music simply being organized sound and silence opens up the possibility for music to be accessible to everyone. It is not only about reading music or analyzing notes, harmony, or melodic lines, although there are many who enjoy doing that. It is about listening and creating sounds, and it also can be about creating symbols to represent the sounds, which links directly into literacy. The text is a symbolic representation of sound. Musical symbols do not need to be notes on a staff; rather, they can be any representation of a sound that makes sense to the composer or those "reading" the score. Wavy lines could indicate wind sounds, or perhaps large asterisk symbols might indicate

"Music has healing power. It has the ability to take people out of themselves for a few hours."

—Elton John (BrainyQuote, n.d.)

thunder. Color can be used as well. A wide blue bar of color at the bottom may indicate an ocean sound. The student or groups of students who create the score will use it as a "map" and read along while they perform. One student may be selected as the "conductor" to help the others know when they need to play. Enjoy the challenge of opening your mind to a broader, more encompassing definition of *music* and see what happens!

Why Does Music Matter?

Our lives begin with listening to the sound of our mother's heartbeat. Inherent in all of us is a rhythm—our personal rhythm. That rhythm connects us to the greater universe and is directly correlated to learning basic literacy skills. Simple childhood nursery rhymes and singing games are the foundational building blocks that set fluency of language in place. Music is often referred to as the soul of a culture or the universal language. It connects people, defines who they are, and naturally builds and strengthens community. Music can inspire us, bring us to tears, calm us, unite us, strengthen us, and connect us with others.

Although music is often taught as a subject outside the general education classroom, it also can be integrated into the classroom curriculum to meet myriad key learning standards. Listening, language development, reading, problem solving, critical thinking, abstract reasoning, patterning, and creative thinking are some of the curriculum goals met through the integration of music. The goals for English language learners, such as developing and expanding modes of expression and communication and developing authentic uses of language, are naturally addressed through music integration, therefore meeting the various needs of all learners in a classroom. Music connects directly to learning language through the use of sound and symbol, reinforcing listening skills, building mathematical concepts of patterning and problem solving, and thinking abstractly.

"Music is the great uniter. An incredible force. Something that people who differ on everything and anything else can have in common."

—Sarah Dessen (2008)

When teachers and students engage in making music together, they create an atmosphere that celebrates the whole and the individual and addresses socially responsive and culturally responsive goals. We work diligently to create classroom environments in which students feel they belong, where they discover their own identity, their approach to learning is honored and supported, and they feel ownership of their learning and a connection to the school community. Integrating music into the curriculum reaches all these goals and more.

Standards

Music in the College and Career Readiness Standards

Musical activities can address standards in language arts, social studies, science, and mathematics, as well as address culturally responsive and social emotional outcomes. In language arts, students can create lyrics to describe using detail, report on a topic, tell a story, or recount an experience. In some cases they will organize their thoughts and use facts and details to describe, and in others they will paraphrase information. In mathematics, music requires students to reason abstractly and quantitatively, generate and analyze patterns, look for and make use of structure, and attend to precision. The science of sound is addressed through instrument construction and listening. Listening and exploring the uses of music across the globe opens doors to a deeper understanding of individual cultures and how, when, and why individuals participate in music-making. Exploring the multiple ways the word *music* is considered and used in various cultures deepens our understanding and broadens our perspectives. For instance, in Ghana, there is no specific word for *percussionist*, *singer*, or *dancer*. The word *music-maker* or *music-making* is used and encompasses all categories of music-making rather than singling out specific areas. Rather than focus on who are the "most talented" musicians, the Ghanaians focus on participation and encourage everyone to participate in making music together.

Exploring Perceptions of Music

Music was established in the Boston schools in 1838, and this may be regarded as the initial introductory period of music in schools across the United States (Birge 1984). With it came the recognition of music specialists who were trained and qualified to teach music. This was beneficial for those specialists, who were finally recognized as worthy additions to a child's education. Music education was now solely the responsibility of the music specialists—the experts. The result of this shift was that many children experienced music education once a week or less.

So it is no surprise that many classroom teachers today lack confidence in their musical ability and choose to engage with students in only a minimal way in musical activities. Most feel comfortable leaving the task of music education to the specialists. If we hope to truly integrate music across the curriculum, ensuring a more comprehensive learning experience, the classroom teacher cannot completely pass the musical baton over to the music specialist. To improve teaching and learning through music integration, we must create a multitude of strategies for integrating the arts whereby every educator, both music specialist and classroom teacher, plays an active part. Everyone must be engaged in music-making at some level.

Because of the current structure, music education is often considered a separate subject and not usually integrated into the classroom curriculum. Our perception of making music, beginning with singing, is often narrowly defined and in most cases continues to be considered, by most educators, to require a great deal of training that involves mastering complicated skills in breathing, vocal technique, diction, and note reading (Pascale 2005). Many classroom teachers feel that they are not proficient enough at singing to teach music in their classrooms. They are happy to put on a CD in the background, but sing? Oh no, leave that to the music specialist. It is difficult to convince many teachers otherwise.

In researching the cultural idea of "singers" and "non-singers," the collected data suggest that, in fact, the categories themselves are a cultural phenomenon (Pascale 2002). Western culture has created the category of "singer." And thus, by default, a "nonsinger" category was created. To qualify as a singer, according to the research, you must, among many things, have confidence; be outgoing, musically expressive, and vocally talented; have a large repertoire of songs; sing in tune; and have a good, strong voice.

This notion of only a select few people being singers is a Western cultural phenomenon and not universal. In an interview, Onika, a Barbadian, said, "Everyone makes music in Barbados. They dance in the streets and sing. When I'm in Barbados singing my music, I am a singer. When I'm in the U.S., I'm not a singer" (Pascale 2005). In Ghana, for example, the distinctions between singer/nonsinger do not exist. *Music*, to Ghanaians, is a general term that refers to drumming, dancing, and singing and is integrated into all aspects of life. It functions as a way to bring people together and convey important cultural, political, and educational messages. Ask a Ghanaian if they are a singer, and they will be perplexed. The question itself makes no sense. Everyone in Ghanaian society is a singer, just as everyone is a dancer and drummer. What holds utmost importance in music-making to Ghanaians is not how well you sing or drum or dance but that you participate. Participation, above all else, is essential, because music-making is about collaboration and relationships (Pascale 2005). As educators, we can take something very important away from this approach.

Bring Music into the Classroom

The challenge for educators is this: Can we begin to embrace an alternative way of thinking about music-making? Is it possible to let go of the notion of the nonsinger and deemphasize musical ability, and, in turn, focus on music-making as a process that builds community and strengthens learning, both of which address culturally responsive and social-emotional learning goals? If so, we open the possibility for creating a school environment where everyone is a musician and everyone is singing. If music in schools is going to continue to flourish and be valued not only as a valuable art form in and of itself, but as an essential learning tool for enhancing curriculum, everyone in the school must participate and be part of the music-making.

Part of this paradigm shift is to open our minds to what we consider music-making to be. For many of us, it means singing, note reading, performing, or mastering an instrument. Let's imagine for a moment that you teach in a school where music is offered weekly solely by the music specialist. That's wonderful and a valuable asset. There are also weekly morning gatherings led by the music specialist that include singing. Where do you fit in as the classroom teacher? How can you support and enhance students' music education? Here are some ideas:

- **Begin by expanding your own perspective of music.** Consider that music-making comes in all forms and is not limited to singing or playing a traditional instrument. Think about music-making in the broadest sense, as organized sound and silence.

- **Teach students to listen.** Explore the idea of sound—found sounds, invented sounds, sounds from the environment, endangered sounds. Encourage students to pay attention to what they hear and discuss their reactions to sound.

- **Focus on participation, not skill building.** Integrating music strengthens community and deepens learning of basic curriculum. It is not about teaching the specific skills of music. It is about honoring everyone in a shared musical experience.

- **Create a safe environment for participation.** Set clear guidelines that allow students (and the teacher!) to participate in music-making and singing without judgment. Begin perhaps by singing with a recording, and then once everyone knows the song, turn the recording off. Remember why you are singing—not to select out the "singers," but rather to use songs to enhance curriculum and build a sense of "ensemble" in the classroom. The emphasis is on community, not on whether every voice is exactly in tune. It means a great deal that everyone participates.

Teach Students to Listen

Oddly enough we often don't consider the most basic component of music and one of the best ways to introduce music to students—listening! How many times a day do educators ask their students to listen? Listening takes practice. If we agree that the basic definition of music is "organized sound and silence," then paying attention to sounds is an essential ingredient. Nothing could be more important than honing a student's listening skills! Begin the process of integrating music by exploring sound and enhancing listening skills.

Children's literacy skills are reinforced when they are read to, or when they hear stories. Children's musical skills also are enhanced by listening. Listening is an activity that is accessible and doable and addresses important core content and standards. Listening builds focus, attention span, discrimination, the ability to categorize or skills in categorization, and much more. It is a wonderful way to begin to integrate music.

Most educators spend an inordinate amount of time asking, if not demanding, that children listen. Many children have stopped listening. They have stopped listening to each other and, usually, have stopped listening to their teachers! And it is no surprise. In today's world, we are bombarded with sound. You can rarely walk into a supermarket, mall, airport, railroad or bus station, hotel, or any other public space without hearing some kind of "music" or announcement blaring from loudspeakers. The sounds of traffic, airplanes, and voices from a crowd envelop us in our daily lives. And with the advent of technology, many of us are attached to our cell phones, earbuds, iPads, and other devices that add to our soundscape. Not only have children stopped listening—we all have. Given the huge number of sounds that surround us daily, we've made careful choices about what we choose to listen to and what we choose to ignore. Unfortunately, for educators, some children have put us on their "ignore" list!

Open students' ears, and your own, with active listening. The Listening Walk activity described here is easy to implement, applicable for any age group, and adaptable for students with varying abilities and for teaching in a hybrid or face-to-face format. Listening exercises are useful to expand vocabulary, particularly for students whose first language is not English. The Listening Walk activity can be adapted in a number of ways. The entire class can go for a listening walk and make note of the sounds they hear during the walk. Or students can take a sound walk at home or in another environment outside of school and share their findings online as well as in person.

Introductory Activity: The Listening Walk

1. **Warm up:** Take two or three minutes in the classroom and ask students to simply stop and listen. Ask them what they hear. Buzzing of fluorescent lights? Paper rustling? Someone coughing? Feet moving? Breathing? This is excellent practice for the next step—the listening walk.

2. **Explain the listening walk:** Explain to students that everyone will now go on a listening walk. Everyone must walk silently, without talking. The only task is to listen—to listen to every sound, including the ones they might be making themselves (heartbeat, jacket rubbing against a pant leg, footsteps, coughing, breathing, and so on). Encourage students to try to remember as many sounds as they can.

3. **Go on the walk:** Once on the walk, tell students they must try to be as quiet as possible. If going outside is not an option, a listening walk inside the school can work very well. Schools are filled with sound! The walk should last five to ten minutes, depending on the group. If the group is capable of it, you could have them take paper and pencil and try writing the sounds they hear. You might want to give very young children an imaginary bag to take with them and have them pretend to put the sounds in the bag. Upon their return, have students take the imaginary sounds out of their bag and describe them. See an example of a sound map on page 105. This activity is easily adaptable as an option to do during free time, at home, or in another setting outside of school.

4. **Back in the classroom:** Once back in the classroom, have students either discuss as a group or write the sounds they heard. Ask them the following questions:

   - What sound was above you? Next to you? Below you?
   - What was the loudest sound? A moving sound? A remarkable sound? A sound that changed direction?
   - What sound would you like to eliminate?
   - What was your favorite sound?
   - What was the most beautiful sound? (Schafer 1992, 31)

Expand and adapt the list of questions to students. The important thing is to focus on listening. Ask students to notice how different the responses may be—everyone went on the same walk, but not everyone heard the same things.

5. **Assessment:** Observe students' participation on the walk and also in the follow-up discussion or writing assignment. Were they able to describe the qualities of the sounds (timbre), the loudness or softness of the sounds (dynamics), and the highness or lowness of the sounds (pitch)? Were they able to describe the sounds they heard? Were they also listening to the responses of others and the group discussion?

The Listening Walk: Curriculum Connections

- **Language arts:** Speaking and listening are two key points of the standards. Through the listening walk, students improve on complex listening skills, not only by doing the exercise of a listening walk, but also by listening to each other's responses. Collecting the sound evidence and writing it down enhances basic writing skills and builds vocabulary. Most often, students describe an object by what it looks like, not what it sounds like. The practice of listening and then finding words to describe sound demonstrates, through writing, their listening experience. To extend the lesson, have students write a narrative piece from the compiled list describing sounds in the environment, take an imaginary listening walk related to a piece of literature, or discuss the meaning of *onomatopoeia* and ask students to create words imitating sounds they heard on the listening walk. They also can write a "sound" poem, using descriptive words from their walk or make a list of the sounds they heard.

- **Social studies:** The listening walk can be adapted and expanded to deepen the understanding of a social studies topic. After completing the listening walk and discussing the sounds students discovered, have them make a list of what they might hear if they were someone in another time and place: a family member traveling in a covered wagon during the Westward movement, an immigrant arriving at Ellis Island, a participant at a traditional American Indian gathering, or a passenger on the Mayflower.

- **Mathematics:** After returning from the listening walk, ask students to list sounds that have a particular pattern, such as high-low-high-low or loud-soft-soft-loud-soft-soft. Have students create symbolic representations of the different sounds and then draw the patterns. Or as a group, classify or categorize sounds by sound type—high, low, soft, loud, natural, metallic, human, wooden, mechanical, and so on. Do some sounds fall into more than one classification? Have students graph the different types of sounds.

- **Science:** Older students can discuss and research the issues of noise pollution. Relate science vocabulary to sound. For example, have students make a list of *extinct* sounds. Ask: "What makes a sound extinct? What are sounds that are *endangered*?" Help students practice tonal discrimination. Ask them to categorize the sounds they heard by tone—high, low, medium. Discuss the concept of *frequency*. As a demonstration, fill water glasses with various amounts of water and ask students to predict whether each glass will make a higher or lower sound when tapped. Or pull a piece of fishing line or wire tight across a big tin can or an open cardboard box. Pluck the string and listen to the sound. Make another "instrument" with a shorter piece of wire. Ask students to predict if the sound will be higher or lower.

- **Visual arts:** After returning from the listening walk, have students choose one location they visited and instruct them to draw the sounds they heard there. Encourage students to draw the sound, not the real image. For example, if they heard wind, they should draw an abstract expression of what the wind in the tree sounded like instead of simply drawing a tree. Ask: "What shape is the sound? What color or colors is the sound? Is it represented with curvy or straight lines?" Have students compare their visual representations. The artist Paul Klee described melody as "taking a tone for a walk." Ask students: "Was there was a sound you heard on the walk that was melodic? Can you sing it? What does it look like?" Have students create a visual representation of a melody using line, shape, and color. Figure 4.1 shows an example of a sound map.

Figure 4.1 Sound Map Example

Sound map created by E. Shea, Newburyport, Massachusetts

Music across the Curriculum

Here are some simple sound and music activities you can use at any grade level. These activities do not require any specialized music knowledge or talent and are easy to implement with minimal preparation.

Sound Diaries

This is an excellent follow-up to the Listening Walk activity. Have students take a few minutes every day to listen to sounds in a particular place. With each listening, students should describe what they hear in a sound diary. Then they can draw the sounds. Ask them: "What do the sounds look like visually? What color are they? What shape are they?" This exercise connects to visual arts elements of line, shape, and color.

Use sound diaries as a tool for expanding vocabulary. Have students write a narrative piece about the sounds they hear, describing more extensively the sounds they notice, what they wonder about, and what listening makes them think about. Adjectives most commonly used by students describe things visually, not through sound. Listening exercises bring an awareness of sound words, which can expand and enhance students' writing and link directly to the language arts curriculum. See Figure 4.2 for an example of a sound diary.

Figure 4.2 Example of a Sound Diary

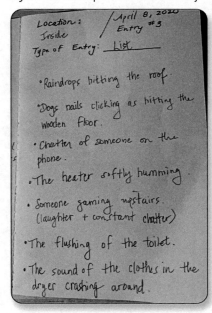

Sound diary created by Hilary DesMarais

Soundscapes

Bring a story, historical event, or particular habitat alive with sound. Have students analyze a particular event or situation purely through sound and then re-create it. Encourage them to carefully select just the essential sounds and place them sequentially in a way that produces an accurate reproduction of the sound environment. Students can re-create sounds with their voices, bodies, and everyday found objects. Many recorded sounds are available on the internet, but the challenge is for students to use found sounds

"A soundscape is a collection of sounds almost like a painting is a collection of visual attractions. When you listen carefully to the soundscape, it becomes quite miraculous."

—R. Murray Schafer
(as cited in New 2009)

or their voices. The audience then listens to the performance with eyes closed, while the performers bring the environment immediately and accurately alive through sound alone. The audience should feel as if they are immersed in the soundscape, whether it is the rain forest, a desert oasis, a space shuttle launch, or a moment in time from a chapter book students are reading. The goal is to re-create the sound of the environment as accurately as possible so that the audience is able to feel they are immersed in it. The creation of soundscapes requires students to create and organize sound symbols, connecting writing, math, and storytelling skills. They also can create an invented musical score or map to follow as they perform. Students can decide how to effectively depict their soundscape. They can color-code it or map it out with symbols. More information about Sound Scores is provided on page 109.

As inspiration or after students have created their soundscapes, watch both the rehearsal and final version of the 2007 Honda commercial where all the car sounds are created with only voices. The rehearsal and the final commercial can be seen on YouTube. (See page 205 for the links.)

Name Rhythms

Begin by having each student clap the syllables of their first and last name, creating a name rhythm. For example, this name has four syllables: Clay/ton/Tal/bert. Have the class echo the "name rhythm."

After hearing and echoing everyone's name, go around the circle again, this time listening to just each name rhythm without echoing. Tell students to listen carefully. Are there name rhythms that have the same rhythmic pattern? For example, Susan Fisher has the same name rhythm as Clayton Talbert.

The name rhythms can then be played on a rhythm instrument. If you don't have access to musical instruments, use found sounds such as tapping a pencil on a notebook, shaking a plastic bottle with paper clips in it, or tapping a ruler. Look around the classroom and find something that will make an interesting sound. Have each student play their name rhythm on an "instrument." Ask students to describe how these sounds differ from their clapping.

Next, have students create a class composition, adding one name rhythm pattern on top of another. The goal of putting all the rhythms together is to create one ensemble, with all the name rhythms interacting. The idea is not to "show off" one name rhythm, but rather to create a group composition where all the name rhythms work together to form a rhythmic piece. Listen to what transpires once all the rhythms are played together. If at first the ensemble falls apart and does not seem to be in sync, that's fine. Stop and analyze how to improve it. The conversation is as important as the exercise itself. What would help to make it better? It might mean that some name rhythms, for the sake of the group ensemble, may need to be slightly adjusted: Clay/ton/Tal/bert may need to become Clay/ton/ /Tal/bert, leaving a longer space between the first two syllables and the last two syllables.

Have students record their name rhythm patterns using symbols. Ask them to draw what they think their name rhythms look like. Figure 4.3 shows an example of name rhythm symbols.

Figure 4.3 Name Rhythm Symbols

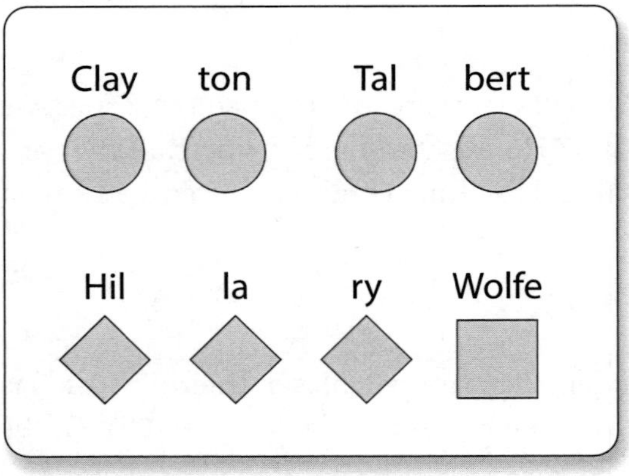

Have students compare and contrast the representations of their name rhythms. Listen for similarities in the rhythms. Is there someone else in the class who has the same name rhythm? Do they look the same? Are there some that are similar but not exactly the same? What's different? Have students play each other's name rhythms, using their drawings as sound scores.

This exercise addresses several important learning standards: recognizing patterns, transferring symbols to sound (a basic literacy skill), developing abstract reasoning skills, developing listening skills, and creating a cooperative group environment.

Sound Scores

To most of us, a familiar musical score consists of notes placed on a staff. This notation is commonly used around the world; however, there are multitudes of ways to notate music. Allowing students to create their own musical score, using their own symbols and scoring techniques, deepens creative and critical-thinking skills and abstract reasoning. A sound score is simply a map that uses symbols to indicate to the reader or "musician" how to play the composition. A sound score also can be created to document sounds. For instance, a rainstorm can be graphically notated with symbols indicating the different sounds (hands rubbing together, clapping, finger snapping, and so on). Figure 4.4 shows an example of a storm sound score.

Figure 4.4 Storm Sound Score

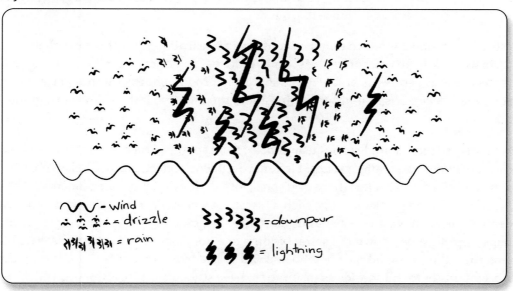

Have students create sound scores, alone or in groups. The compositions could connect to any curriculum content—social studies, science, math, or language arts. For example, students could create sound scores representing a tornado, a walk through the rain forest, or a crucial moment in a novel.

Sound Exploration

Ask students to bring in interesting sounds from home. Tell them they are not looking for an instrument, but rather an everyday object they can use to make an interesting sound. If it is difficult for students to bring in something from home, they also can use classroom objects (rulers, pencils, trash cans, erasers, notebooks, and so on) to make interesting sounds, or you can bring a collection of found sounds from home. Have students demonstrate their sounds and explain why they chose them. Then have them describe their sounds using sound words such as *loud*, *soft*, *metallic*, *percussive*, *natural*, or *electronic*.

Ask each student to discover three different ways to play their found object so it makes three different sounds. For instance, a student could scrape a pencil on a cheese grater; tap the pencil on the outside of the grater, making a different kind of sound; or put the pencil inside the cheese grater and move it around.

"Music . . . touches us both intelligently and emotionally. . . . [As] the needs of our students constantly change, we find ourselves needing to explicitly teach the social and emotional strategies our students lack. Listening to music can do just that!"

—Elizabeth Peterson
(2018, para. 2–3)

Use students' found sounds to enhance content-area learning. Have them use their mathematical skills to categorize the sounds. Notice if some sounds fall into more than one category. Have students organize the sounds in groups, choose rhythm patterns, and create a whole-class or small-group composition, then represent the sounds in a graph or chart.

Have students create sound stories using their found sounds. You can do this exercise in a large group or in smaller groups. First, have students determine what else those sounds remind them of. Then, have everyone close their eyes while one student plays their sound in some particular way, such as scraping a pencil across a cheese grater. Ask students to think of what else it sounds like—maybe a motor starting up or a pig grunting! Perhaps running a pen down the spiral binding of a notebook may sound like a little bug. Hitting the palm of a hand on a notebook could sound like someone walking. Using these interpretations of found sounds as inspiration, have students create a story in which the sounds are used as sound effects. This exercise reinforces abstract thinking, helps students visualize the story, and builds creativity and imagination.

Songwriting

The availability of educational materials on the internet provides more than enough songs to supplement any and every curriculum subject. Although these songs are often clever and can definitely support student learning, to make learning truly relevant and meaningful, let students play a role in the creative aspect of songwriting. Creating and singing a song reinforces learning. We know this inherently because many adults still sing the ABC song or recite "Thirty days hath September" without hesitation. *In Critical Links: Learning in the Arts and Student Academic and Social Development*, editor Richard Deasy (2002) cites several research studies documenting how music-making increases spatial reasoning and spatial temporal reasoning, motivates writing and language arts skills, and improves language for learners of English.

When students write a song, they have ownership of it and are much more apt to remember it. It is perfectly acceptable to use a standard familiar melody when creating a new song. Having students engage in the songwriting process is ultimately more satisfying and, beyond reinforcing their learning, enhances their creativity, imagination, and cooperative skills. As always, the process itself is a valuable endeavor. Having students create their own songs about their learning reinforces language arts skills, as well as skills related to the content area the song focuses on.

The easiest approach to songwriting is to have students write lyrics to a melody they are familiar with. These tunes are usually melodies they've heard as young children, which are easily adapted to new lyrics, such as "Old MacDonald Had a Farm," "Skip to My Lou," and "Row, Row, Row Your Boat." Or perhaps the song is one from another country. Students can choose any melody that is familiar to everyone or easily learned. The important thing is to let students make that choice.

Chants

In addition to creating songs about a particular subject matter, have students create a non-melodic chant. It is the most effective way to remember something. Chants can be made up about any topic—the water cycle, names of the continents, long and short vowels, rules of long division, or classroom rules. All that is needed is rhythm and, if desired, rhyme. Rap is a well-known genre, and many students are quite comfortable creating chants using rap rhythms.

Here is an excellent example of when and how to effectively implement the chant strategy. Emily Matunis, a middle school teacher from Massachusetts, designed a lesson using chants with the following goals and objectives: 1) acquire key vocabulary and comprehend the three types of complex waves associated with earthquakes; 2) experiment with and use a variety of tempos and pitches to create a cohesive change; 3) cooperate and collaborate with others in creating the chant; and 4) encourage hesitant classmates to participate in a performance. This lesson addressed state science and arts standards. Students created chants and added movement for each section to help them remember all the facts.

Making Instruments

Students can make many simple instruments with found materials. (Refer to Appendix D: Recommended Resources for books on instrument making.) Students explore myriad sounds when making their own instruments. This exercise can relate to science, math, and language arts. The properties of sound, sound waves, and vibration are all addressed in instrument making; this includes both science and mathematics curricula as well as patterning, listening, and analyzing sound properties. Descriptive words that describe the sound of the instrument can lead to poems, narratives, or stories, thus integrating music into language arts. Exploring onomatopoeia is another natural outcome of instrument making, as is exploring metaphor and simile. For example, you can make and play with a rain stick. Have everyone listen. Ask students to write a poem describing the sound. Ask: "What does the rain stick sound like to you? Does it remind you of something, such as a rainstorm or an ocean? Or is it a whoosh of sounds—*tap, tap, tap, swish, swish, swish*?" Encourage students to explore the possibilities. Or have them create their own wind chimes from natural objects. Read Seamus Heaney's poem "The Rain Stick" (1993) as a beautiful example of onomatopoeia and descriptive, rhythmic verse. Suggest that students write their own poem, beginning with Heaney's first line: "Upend the rain stick and what happens next is . . ." as C. DeFilipp did with her poem.

Upend the rain stick and what happens next
Is the tumultuous downpour of unfettered gravity
Interior bits falling to their final destination with
Newton's law pulling at them
All that is inside and up cascades to its down
In a furious rush of sound bites, swooshing
And flying, like Angel Falls or something less
Extravagant . . . draining water
Upend the rain stick and what happens next is
Inevitability, that all that is high will at some point
Be low, and all that is quiet, given the correct agitation
Will roar with thunder.

Poem and rain stick created by C. DeFilipp, Maine

Sound Effect Stories

When reading books aloud to students, add sounds to enhance the story. Sounds can be verbal or created using found objects in the classroom. For example, when the billy goats are trip-trapping over the bridge, use your feet or hands to make stomping or tapping noises. If a doorbell rings, sing out "ding-dong." On subsequent readings, have students provide the soundtrack. Students also can create songs and chants based on the story, or they can use the actual words from the book. Add sound effects to nonfiction content-area reading as well. If the class is reading about frogs, have students make frog noises. When reading about tornadoes, a large whooshing noise is appropriate. Be sure to have a nonverbal "stop" signal in place to bring a quick end to the sounds. *Bringing the Rain to Kapiti Plain* is an excellent book to use for adding sounds and movement.

Singing Games

There are many playground chants, clapping games, and traditional singing games that provide wonderful insight into a specific culture. As part of a social studies unit, research traditional games and songs to enhance the understanding of the culture or period being studied. Jump-rope rhymes are part of many cultures. It is important to research as much as possible about where the game is played and who typically plays it and why. Of course it is ideal if students or their parents or grandparents can share games, stories, or songs from their particular culture. Refer to the music resources in Appendix D for more information.

Traditional Folk Songs

Folk or traditional songs provide a rich resource for understanding culture, tradition, and history to enhance a social studies curriculum. There are many resources that provide songs from different cultures, as well as songs from U.S. history, such as the Civil War and Revolutionary War, songs about building the railroad, songs written by women in the mills—the possibilities are endless. The website **www.folkstreams.net** was developed by a nonprofit dedicated to finding, preserving, and contextualizing documentary films on American traditional cultures. Search the term "music films" on the website, and you will find a wealth of resources.

Many books and websites include music from every region of the United States and from around the world, from ballads to spirituals. These sources give students authentic insight into a particular period of history. The Smithsonian Folkways website, **folkways.si.edu**, is "dedicated to supporting cultural diversity and increased understanding among peoples through the documentation, preservation, and dissemination of sound." The site provides recordings and lesson plans. Begin by having students read the lyrics of a song, analyzing what the songwriter is trying to convey about their condition. Quite often, as in the case of the Revolutionary War, students can compare two songs that express two different points of view. Decolonizing the Music Room (**decolonizingthemusicroom.com**) offers videos, podcasts, and lists of resources from a wide range of cultures.

Concluding Thoughts

Music-making creates a more humanistic, caring community that encourages recognizing, listening to, and celebrating every voice. Our schools, now more diverse than ever, must have spaces made for individual and community voices to be recognized and honored. Nick Page (1995b) claims that making music together helps "democratize" the community, giving everyone an opportunity to become the leader and feel ownership. Once this mindset is embraced, enormous possibilities open up, not only for music but for all the arts: dance, poetry, visual arts, and drama. There is much to gain once we rid ourselves of the limiting categories such as singer/nonsinger, dancer/nondancer, or artist/non-artist. When cultural and societal boundaries are broken down, minds are released and creativity is enlisted (Pascale 2006).

Music-making, in all its iterations, brings people together, builds community, and creates a sense of belonging and common purpose, both to celebrate the diversity of music expression that characterizes the human condition and to suggest that music-making is open to all. The focus should not be on a hierarchy of talent, where one singer is superior to another, but rather should be on the communal voice (Page 1995b). Equally important, music-making strengthens learning and provides for assessment of students in innovative ways that recognize learning differences. Integrating music teaches students, at the most basic level, to listen, correct, and pursue excellence (Page 1995b). Including musical activities as part of the teaching and learning palette strengthens student learning. It is most certainly not about whether we sing beautifully or in tune or read notes perfectly from a musical score. It is about creating a learning environment that stimulates and engages students with excitement, connection, and relevance.

As educators, we are stimulated by the challenge of teaching students who all have a great potential to learn. Our task is to investigate each student's abilities through multiple lenses so that each reaches their full potential. Integrating music into the curriculum offers a powerful option for learning.

Reflection

1. What is your musical culture? What songs did you grow up singing, or what music did you or your family listen to? What would play on your personal musical jukebox?

2. How varied is the musical culture of students in your classroom? How can you honor those differences?

3. What do you notice when students participate in a musical activity, like singing or creating a chant? What changes in the room? Do you notice a change in how students connect with content when music is introduced?

4. Choose one content–area lesson you plan to teach in the next month. How can you integrate music into teaching the content?

Visual Art: Accessing Content through Image

Visual Art: Accessing Content through Image

What Is Visual Art?

Visual Arts "include the traditional fine arts such as drawing, painting, printmaking, photography, and sculpture; media arts including film, graphic communications, animation, and emerging technologies; architectural, environmental, and industrial arts such as urban, interior, product, and landscape design; folk arts; and works of art such as ceramics, fibers, jewelry, works in wood, paper, and other materials" (National Art Education Association n.d.).

Communication through human mark-making is a universal and ancient activity that has deep diverse roots, influences, and meaning in many cultures (Schaefer-Simmern 2003). We experience the world through images—seeing and reading images and making marks before we read words. We create images to make sense of our world. Visual art reflects the world we live in. Art can help us understand our own lives, cultures, and experiences, as well as the experiences of others. We can understand history and historic cultures by the art left behind. Art not only reflects but also shapes our cultural narrative over time. Artists have raised questions, commented, and investigated new ideas through images. Artist and activist Favianna Rodriguez notes that art is a universal language that fosters emotional connection: "Art is uniquely able to speak to our understanding of the world by delivering potent, powerful and empathetic content. People engage with art in a very different way than they engage with a policy paper or a news article or even a protest" (Brooks 2017).

"Being intentional about the images you use in class is an easy thing to do, but it has a profound impact on classroom culture. When students see themselves reflected in the lesson, they are more invested in what they are learning."

—Lidia Aguirre (2020, para. 8)

F. Robert Sabol writes "We continuously are inundated with innumerable visual images and messages on television, computers, digital communications devices, and in the printed media. Neuroscience has shown that a significant portion of the human brain is devoted to understanding visual stimulation and to decoding visual messages we receive through our sense of vision" (2011).

Why Does Visual Art Matter?

Art is part of our everyday world, influencing and inspiring us. How can we create more opportunities where we are taught to create, observe, and analyze our visual culture?

"'Art,' a high school student told me, 'has the ability to affect people in ways nothing else can. For me, I've found art as a way to express what I'm feeling without even knowing it at the time. Art helps me understand my own life.'"

—Kathryn Fishman-Weaver (2019)

The visual arts are a natural fit in the classroom as an integrated approach to many non-art subjects. Drawing can improve our ability to focus and notice details in ways that enhance curiosity and observation skills (Bensusen 2020). Reading is enhanced by the creation of mental images. We see students who are stumped about what to write; yet when they engage with images, their writing becomes filled with ideas and rich details. Science is dependent on observation. In mathematics, visualizing patterns is key. The use of images in the classroom creates a way to translate, communicate, and draw from the world. As you think about your next lesson, why not begin with looking (Vivian Poey, pers. comm.)?

Students learn by making art and by observing the work of others. Invite students to create and respond to works of art, and to draw ideas from their experiences, encounters, and observations in the world. In this chapter we will explore a variety of ways for students to engage with developing knowledge and skills about visual art, as well as how to describe their artistic choices and decipher choices in the work of others, and discover ways to express themselves and consider the functions of art in our visual culture.

Growing data show that visual arts improve academic achievement. The arts level the classroom playing field through their inherent differentiation and universality. The arts, and in this case the visual arts, offer a nontext, visual entry into content and provide student participants (and teachers) multiple ways to show evidence of learning. "Teaching Literacy Through Art," a study conducted by the Guggenheim Museum, found that visual arts education enhanced literacy skills (Korn 2012). "The study found that students in the program performed better in six categories of literacy and critical thinking skills—including thorough description, hypothesizing, and reasoning—than did students who were not in the program" (Kennedy 2006). In *Studio Thinking 2: The Real Benefits of Arts Education,*

Standards

Visual Arts in the College and Career Readiness Standards

Visual literacy is an integral part of the standards. With the addition of teaching standards for Digital Arts Media and the option of many schools to offer remote delivery models, it has become critical that all students also be technologically proficient. By responding to text in visual representations, students make logical inferences from text, determine central ideas or themes, and interpret words and phrases (particularly figurative meanings). Students also integrate and evaluate content presented in visual formats and text. Through visual art, students can show their understanding of complex literary and informational texts. When critiquing their own visual work or the work of others, students can express their ideas clearly and persuasively, build on others' ideas, present supporting evidence, and evaluate information presented visually.

Hetland et al. (2013) further expanded on the eight "studio habits of mind" developed by students taking arts classes: develop craft, engage and persist, envision, express, observe, reflect, stretch and explore, and understand the art world. Clearly students can benefit by working with visual art in the classroom, learning skills and knowledge in both visual arts and the curricular content they're exploring.

Studies suggest that integrating art across the curriculum can help with comprehension and engagement (Mathieson 2015) and long-term retention (Rinne, Gregory, and Yarmolinkskaya 2011). Integrating visual art that reflects students in your classroom is one way to foster appreciation of our similarities and differences across cultures and traditions.

Observation and Interpretation of Visual Images

Every curricular theme has a visual aspect to it. Students can draw from the visual world to enhance what they are studying in the school curriculum. Visuals are open-ended in ways words are not and can prompt students to notice and make meaning. There is a lot of information embedded in an image, and this can add to and deepen classroom investigations. Working with images in this way will inevitably enhance writing. If you think about it, description is a visual thing. When students work with visuals, their writing will have access to rich details and characteristics of the image (Robert Shreefter, pers. comm.).

Observation is central to working with visual art. Begin with visual narrative and then move into language narrative. Create images and ask students to add words. This allows students to draw on their own observations. Observation is contextual by nature, so situating the image in the context of the curriculum being studied makes a difference (Robert Shreefter, pers. comm.).

Production of Visual Images

When students are allowed to select from a variety of materials and use the elements of art to convey meaning, making art can be a form of active learning and a way to synthesize ideas, as well as a form of assessment as they "show what they know." Provide students with opportunities to explore a range of art materials and processes to create their own images. Offer direct experiences with paint, clay, drawing tools, photographs, textured papers, and other media. As students make choices about how they use materials to communicate, they use higher-order thinking skills, such as analysis and evaluation. Students think about how best to work with materials at hand to visually represent an idea.

Students can work with the elements of visual art—line, form, shape, color, texture, and pattern—to make meaning and construct ideas. They need to make choices about colors or lines, for example, and then explain their choices (Vivian Poey, pers. comm.). As students

create, they draw information from a range of sources and use the elements of art to express their ideas about that information. The elements of art are tools with which students construct meaning. Students learn about the elements as they create.

Visual representation is applicable to every content area. Students can use clay to construct vessels built from geometric shapes, learn about perimeter through sculpture, and tie visual art to math goals by making abstract concepts concrete. Students' comprehension and descriptive writing are enhanced when they create storyboards to show the progression of a fairy tale they are creating. Moving between image and text as students represent their understanding of significant moments in a story can enrich descriptive details as students draw ideas from their paintings. Students are called to use their imaginations to create new ideas, use materials in a two- or three-dimensional space to communicate those ideas, and show they have met developmental benchmarks and curricular standards.

Visual art experiences allow students to use art as their own language. Because there are no formulaic rules, as there are in writing, visual art allows students who do not draw well or who do not yet have knowledge of the elements of art to participate. The trick for the teacher is to ease students into using their imaginations, to allow them to understand that trial and error is a natural part of the process and that art is a mode of expression defined by each individual.

How is what is in their heads different from the visual art they create? Often there is a "happy accident" or a difference between what was planned and how it came out. Art can be exciting, because students do not know what they are going to get; it is new. In visual art, it is the making itself that is key (Robert Shreefter, pers. comm.). The creative process allows students to work from the same instructions but present their learning through different interpretations. In this way, students learn from one another and bring forward their own unique translations while demonstrating their content learning.

Introductory Activity: Storyboarding

Here is an introductory lesson to get students thinking visually. Students create a series of images based on curricular content. Tell them they will create a storyboard to share ideas about a concept. This could include a sequential story (beginning, middle, end), the description of a scientific process (chemical reaction, the path of the circulatory system, growth of a seed into a plant), or the factors that led to a historical moment. Working from images allows students to first work metaphorically, and their writing will be more richly descriptive as a result.

1. **Planning sketch:** Decide how many panels students will need to create a visual narrative. Fold and then unfold large newsprint paper so the folds create square or rectangular sections for individual sketches. Ask students to use the newsprint panels as a place to develop ideas and sketch rough thumbnail images in pencil that will be fully developed in the final storyboard. Explain to students that the planning process is different from implementing final ideas. They are not replicating content twice. Rather, they are identifying and developing ideas on newsprint, and then they will manifest the fully developed ideas in the final storyboard. Ask students in their planning phase to experiment with layout so they are thinking about how they are using the space in each panel.

2. **Storyboard:** Once students have created thumbnail sketches or drafts of their storyboards, they can use those plans to create their final ideas. At this point they can add words to the images. This prompts students to move between image and text, which draws out new ideas. Give students choices about how they want to

depict their visual narrative; not all students are comfortable drawing. Tell them they can take photographs, use images from online sources or magazines, paint abstract shapes, or use found materials to create a collage. The focus should be on conveying a sequence of ideas, not the exact medium.

3. **Sharing:** Ask students to share their storyboards, discussing what they created, what they learned in the process, the choices they made, and how they are investigating the curricular concept.

4. **Feedback:** Ask the rest of the class to talk about what they see in the storyboards. Ask: "What do you find interesting? What made you think? How are they are similar to or different from choices you made in your own storyboard?" (Robert Shreefter, pers. comm.).

The sequencing of visual images is an organizing and idea-generating strategy for more structured writing activities as well. Teacher Stacy Winterfeld notes, "I have learned . . . that struggling writers may benefit from creating storyboards prior to writing their ideas down on paper. By first creating and viewing images, they then may be more successful in developing the words and sentences needed to describe what they want to say. . . . By sketching out their ideas, we are allowing our students a much higher chance of success and creativity with their writing, while also allowing them to potentially dig much deeper and think much more critically than they may otherwise have been doing" (pers.comm.).

Visual Art Strategies

There are many ways to introduce visual art into your curriculum. Here are a few flexible, easy-to-implement strategies.

Visual Essay

Assign or allow students to choose a curricular concept and provide time for them to find related images from a variety of sources: internet, magazines, discarded books, and so on. Then have students choose and sequence the images to tell a story. Students can add language or writing to their presentation of images. Have students create an exhibit of their visual works, create books, or present their images in blogs or websites. Encourage them to look analytically at each image, questioning what is noticeable and what is not. Have students present their visual essays to the group to view, discuss, and describe what is there or what is suggested.

Observational Drawing

Observational drawing is a heightened way of observing. Have students closely observe items related to a curricular area of study, such as leaves, rocks, or flowers (science); tessellations or Mandelbrot sets (mathematics); or historical artifacts or art (social studies). Ask them to draw what they see. The focus should be less on getting a beautiful drawing and more on close observation, as long as students are representing details they observe. Working visually cultivates the development of deep observation skills and an interest in noticing detail. This attention to detail can then translate into students' writing.

"When you draw, you learn to see the world completely differently. Sketches allow you to notice closely and document details. You realize that the world is not made out of lines, that white is not white—it's purple or green and it changes when the light hits. Asking students to document their learning visually can allow students to focus in on details, and discover based on their own observations" (Vivian Poey, pers. comm.).

Collage

Provide students with a variety of collage materials (textured material, colored paper, origami paper, found objects such as leaves) and have students construct visual representations of curricular concepts. Encourage students to experiment with different ways to put the materials together, considering color, shape, textures, and meaning. Have students observe what others have done, which will spark new ideas for their own work. Hold a discussion of one another's work, and have students respond in oral language or writing. Invite students to explore the layering and/or juxtaposition of artistic elements and to compose their collage applying the principles of design (see page 165).

Mixed Media

Invite students to work with a range of media, such as clay, paint, colored pencils, and technologies, to produce visual work based

Collage created by Dana Schildkraut based on a science lesson about genetics.

on curricular content. These materials can provide students with new ways to create a visual response to content, represent their understanding of an idea, or investigate a concept as an exploration. With the use of accessible video and sound recordings, students can create their own stories, reach more people, and feel part of a global community. The use of technology supports inclusion of students of all abilities and provides a wealth of new tools that support all students showing what they know (Creegan-Quinquis and Thormann 2017).

Visual Arts across the Curriculum

Like all the arts, visual art is flexible enough to be used across the curriculum. Between testing and worksheets, you may worry that there is not time for this kind of in-depth work. Yet there are ways to structure your classroom to integrate visual art to deepen learning. Show visual images to students to provide context or provoke discussion about a unit. Ask students to express their understanding in a visual response. Have students keep visual journals with sketches, cut-out images, and photographs to demonstrate their ideas and stimulate writing. You will find that for many students, working visually enhances their writing with more descriptive language. Hubbard argues, "Children's drawings are viable tools for problem solving. Through them children make sense of the world and impart their visions. Teachers who channel children narrowly toward verbal solutions may be denying them the opportunity to share the full power of their images" (1987, 60).

Visual Art in Mathematics

Incorporating visual imagery into your math lessons can help make mathematical concepts tangible. For example, kindergarten and first-grade students can work on number concepts by drawing addition and subtraction story problems or creating them through sculpture. Cut sponges or potatoes into geometric shapes and have students dip them into paint and stamp repeating patterns such as AB, ABAB, or ABCABC. This helps make an abstract math concept concrete and can illustrate student learning (Susan Fisher, pers. comm.).

Have students explore the idea of symmetry by creating tessellations, designs in which a shape is repeated to form a pattern. Students can use pen and ink on paper or use collage, in which they must paste shapes together on the picture plane in symmetrical balance. This activity requires students to plan and measure carefully and solve practical mathematical problems (Kerrie Bellisario, pers. comm.). Check out a library book on folding origami and have students create origami animals to investigate angles and fractions. A lotus fold, for instance, the basis for most origami, is folded in half, then quarters, and then eighths.

A complex activity can address multiple standards at once. Have students create a self-portrait soft-sculpture puppet. Have students create their own rulers, use them to measure in the initial planning stages, and use a protractor to find the circumference of a circle, which becomes the pattern for the puppet's head. Then have students determine the radius of the circle and weigh stuffing on a scale. Have students document their thinking and creative process in a work portfolio. Display the puppets along with students' written explanations of the mathematical concepts. In addition to providing a hands-on and engaging entry into the study of mathematics, this lesson allows for meaningful dialogue with students about their own abilities and how math concepts are used in their lives (Dr. Maureen Creegan-Quinquis, pers. comm.).

Visual Art in Science

Observation is key to scientific understanding. Use visual art to focus and expand student observations. Have students observe and draw scientific processes. For example, have them plant seeds and document in images what they notice at each stage of growth, as well as what they imagine will happen next. To kick off a study of light, have students paint the sky at different times of the day, observing and documenting what they see with paint.

Begin a unit of study with deep observation (Poey, pers. comm.). Focus on observation by asking students to create a drawing of an object, and then use a viewfinder (a square cut out of paper) to zoom in on their subject. Have students draw or paint the smaller, detailed view, noticing finer details, color, and value. Then have them zoom in even more and transform what they see into abstract shapes, as if they were looking through a microscope. Finally, have students create a science newsletter featuring these drawings and students' writings about the progression of their observations (Kerrie Bellisario, pers. comm.).

Watercolor Tools, S. Fisher, Adjunct Faculty, Lesley University

This focus on deepening observation skills can be transferred to different areas of science. Have students keep a nature journal, first sketching what they see in the environment, then describing their observations with words. Middle school students can use a visual journal to track their discoveries during dissection labs.

Visual art integration also involves opening students' eyes to the fact that visual art has always been a part of the other disciplines. Painting involves understanding the chemistry of pigments and chemicals to achieve colors; photography involves the chemical components of developing a picture; and drawing and painting involve preparing raw materials as well as measurement, perspective, and patterning (Susan Fisher, pers. comm.). Have students use real-world science in visual art to explore scientific concepts.

The materials used to create visual art can provide hands-on experiences with scientific principles. Watercolors are clean and easy to work with to explore cause and effect. Just put a dollop of watercolor from a tube on a plate and let it dry—this will give you enough paint to use for two lessons. Allow students to experiment with laying down crayon color and painting watercolor over it (wax resist). Have students sprinkle salt onto wet watercolors, where it will crystallize and create patterns. Have students observe and document these changes and processes closely and then use students' experiences as an introduction to the scientific principles involved. These experiments also can enhance learning in visual art. When students are allowed to play with materials, they discover new possibilities and then use this information when creating compositions (Susan Fisher, pers. comm.).

Visual art also can be a synthesizing activity and a form of assessment in science. Have students create a photomontage of scientific processes such as decay or states of matter. Have them apply their research of habitat by creating pop-up books that illustrate the flora and fauna that exist in different geographic zones. Visual representations of understanding can serve as a great assessment tool to show what students have learned in their research.

Visual Art in Social Studies

Observing art (photographs, films, painting, collage, sculpture, drawings, carvings, and so on) from many cultures can serve as a jumping-off point for discussions about an era, a

movement, a historic event, or the portrayal of a culture. Viewing multiple modes of work by diverse groups of artists can be a great way to set the stage for work in the classroom. These artists can inspire and serve as examples of people who create, but their work also provides ways into writing and research. Mural artist Judy Baca, for example, works with historical traditions in mural-making, drawing from the community for inspiration. Installation artist Fred Wilson creates museum installations that question who is represented and who is not. Collage artist

Mural image by Alex Edgerly.

Romare Bearden documents the areas where he lived and worked, capturing African American culture in the 1930s. Viewing a wide range of artists' work can spark student projects that allow them to engage in similar explorations through visual mediums.

Free resources, such as government photo archives, provide a wealth of visual information. For example, the Works Progress Administration (WPA) and the Farm Security Administration (FSA) put unemployed artists to work during the Great Depression to document every facet of American life. They created one of the largest photo collections in the world, which is available online for free through the Library of Congress website.

Students can create visual works based on their own lived experiences as well. Have students create neighborhood maps, including where they live and three different places of interest. Then, have students map out their paths to get from one place to another. Students should use different lines, textures, and colors to represent different areas of their maps.

In the Classroom

Visual art can help students make personal connections to curriculum. Former fifth-grade educator Berta Berriz, who taught English learners in Boston used an arts-based approach to biography/autobiography writing that attempts to build a direct bridge from the biography of a character from early U.S. history to students' lives. Each student created a book illustrating a significant moment in the life of a historical figure. The art provided language for representing this moment. These turning points reflected students' feelings about their own diverse experiences and journeys. For example, one student chose Squanto's experience learning English, which was parallel to his own learning of a new language. Another student chose Sacajawea's entry into another culture, which mirrored the student's own journey. Students selected one event in their character's life to depict in a pop-up book. Deepening their knowledge of one event supported students in constructing time lines—a string of events in a life. Students placed their biography time lines on a larger time line of U.S. history. They paired up with Time Line Buddies for discussion throughout the writing process. The teacher reflected on how students worked collaboratively: "One student quickly became our tree expert, teaching others; another was an expert at drawing the figure; and yet another [became an expert] at some of the engineering skills necessary for making 3D work and conceptualizing one scene in three rows of the book. Concepts such as foreground, mid-ground, background as well as scale and grounding elements, etc., were considered. Text-illustration congruence was also discussed. Some of the students' moments were really a period in a figure's life. How could a student choose only one moment—and which moment would be most crucial to represent? Our biographer of Squanto asked the class for help. Should he have Squanto sitting at a desk learning English? Or should Squanto, now having learned English, be addressing his people? After much consideration, Squanto was to be placed on the deck of the ship to represent his leaving London to return to America. This solution not only pinpointed this moment but it spoke to his time in England, his need to return to America, and symbolized the great journey he had taken. This and other discussions became the key aspect in having students collaborate, learn about each other's figures, and piece together strategies for both easy and very complex issues of representation and use of symbols" (Donovan, Shreefter, and Adams 2005).

Visual Art in Language Arts

Visual arts can support emerging writers. Working in the visual arts allows students to create and decode another type of language—metaphors that reflect their ideas and understanding. Students can create images that stand for ideas that are symbolic, and they can discover what happens when they move from image to text. Coming up with an image first is often easier than writing cold (Robert Shreefter, pers. comm.). Conversely, when students are asked to write first and then translate the ideas from their writing into visual images, they are analyzing text, problem solving, and making critical decisions as they decide what images to use (Kerrie Bellisario, pers. comm.).

Begin by asking students to maintain visual journals in which they keep observational sketches. Shreefter says that when students begin to think using both languages (visual and written), they benefit in both areas. He notes, "The creation of art allows students to create their own language for expressing who they are and what they know. They can use classroom texts along with their own languages and experiences for writing and art making" (Robert Shreefter, pers. comm.). Have students create visual essays on any topic of study or have them create books to visually document their personal ideas about curricular content or their lives.

In the book *In the Middle*, Nancie Atwell, a pioneer of responsive teaching in literacy, describes the adverse effects of taking a one-size-fits-all approach to teaching (1998). Atwell states, "Student participants in the intermediate grades begin to seek reassurances that what they do is acceptable to others. They become aware of audience—of others' opinions and realize that what they've done will be judged" (1998, 148). This is why it becomes critical to create safe spaces in which educators can implement inclusive visual arts integration strategies that help ease the anxiety (Willcox 2017).

In the Classroom

Educator Kerrie Bellisario worked with her high school students to explore using media to create new ideas during Banned Books Week. One of her students isolated one hundred words from *To Kill a Mockingbird* by Harper Lee to remix into a new image.

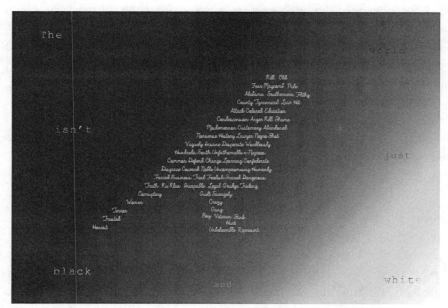

Art created by Neel Badlani

In the Classroom

Dr. Maureen Creegan-Quinquis uses a process-based art-integration approach to teach writing that builds on the work of Susan Sheridan. Sheridan suggests that teachers can use blind contour drawing as an entry point into writing, which can be particularly useful for English language learners (Sheridan 1997, 5). The blind contour technique asks students to draw without looking, critiquing, or erasing the drawing, preventing students from being paralyzed with self-consciousness and preventing too much self-critiquing as they draw. In this technique the drawing is not analyzed as it is created, which facilitates a smoother translation from what the student observes to what is put on the paper.

Creegan-Quinquis asks students to draw a natural artifact, such as a leaf, in pencil without looking at what they are drawing until it is finished. As students draw the leaf without looking at the lines they are making, focusing fully on the leaf as they draw, they are asked to think about how they would describe the marks they have made. Is the line smooth? Is the edge of the leaf wiry? Students are asked to note the type of lines that emerge. When they are finished drawing, they write words that describe the lines they have made. In doing this, they are cataloguing visual information. Students then work in pairs or small groups to compare and discuss their word choices. They begin with words they feel they can use for an entry into writing and then work with each other to expand the vocabulary. These new vocabulary words and descriptors can become seeds for poetry, stories, or other writings.

The watercolor triptych strategy is another way to connect visual arts to several curriculum areas and social-emotional learning (SEL). The strategy allows students to explore color, watercolor techniques, and emotions, which supports SEL, language arts, science, and math. Begin by teaching different watercolor techniques (find "Watercolor Techniques for Kids" on YouTube for examples of techniques). Give students time to experiment and explore to discover how to use the brush and different amounts of water and paint. Students can use craypas and crayons (using the side of the crayon) if watercolors are not available. After students experiment, discuss the ways color can connect to emotions and feelings. The students then fold their paper into thirds and create a three-part emotion painting. This project creates a perfect opportunity to write stories or poetry about one or more of the emotions depicted on their triptych.

Watercolor Emotion Triptych

(Left to right—confused, happy, sad)

S. Fisher, Adjunct Faculty, Lesley University

Concluding Thoughts

Encouraging students to explore ideas through the making of images allows them to tap into thoughts, feelings, and responses that may be elusive in written or spoken word on the first try. King and Ippolito argue that "lingustic knowledge cannot completely explain or describe what we know, and trying to verbalize our thoughts and feelings frequently obstructs the self-discovery process" (2001, 71). Drawing and creating images allow students to explore their ideas in new forms. Karen Gallas reflects on the use of drawing as a way to understand

insects in her classroom: "Knowing wasn't just telling something back as we had received it. Knowing meant transformation and change. . . . For both children and teacher, the arts offer opportunities for reflection upon the content and the process of learning and they foster a deeper level of communication about what knowledge is and who is truly in control of the learning process" (1991, 50). Allowing students to move between "languages" of text and image provides new ways for students to explore, relate to, and express ideas.

The fact that each student produces something different through their own interpretation of the content is important. Part of the art-making process involves looking closely at one another's work and appreciating the choices. It allows everyone in the classroom to appreciate the work rather than evaluating based on a hierarchical idea of the right answer. "When we use our own experience . . . I learn about you, you learn about me or about the students in the first row. The other way we always assume the teacher has the answer and that we have to find out what it is. One of the things about art-making and about appreciation of other art is just that. We become appreciators rather than people who know or don't know. We become people who are excited about learning about and from each other, even if we don't agree. Which is a lot different from not knowing the answers" (Robert Shreefter, pers. comm.). This is a different kind of learning where students have more control of knowledge and how they work with it.

Reflection

1. Where might the use of illustration heighten observation skills in your curriculum?

2. What artist exemplars might serve as catalysts to deepen a curricular topic?

3. When students work with different materials (paint, clay, oil sticks, found objects), how does the way they express their ideas change?

Creative Movement as a Learning Process

Creative Movement as a Learning Process

[F]rom infancy onwards we interpret the world not just intellectually, but through our senses, our physical intelligence.

—Robin Grove, Catherine Stevens, and Shirley McKechnie (2005)

Children are natural movers. When they are asked to sit for long periods of time, their brains disconnect. Fidgeting begins . . . minds wander. Bringing movement into the classroom stimulates brain activity, preparing students for deeper learning throughout the day. As Susan Griss, choreographer, teaching artist, and Lesley University Creative Arts in Learning adjunct faculty member, notes, "Children naturally move. They react to and explore the world in physical ways. No one has to teach them to jump for joy, to roll down a grassy hill, or to pound their bodies on the floor during a tantrum. When they arrive in elementary school, they are fluent in this nonverbal, physical language. However, rather than using this natural resource by channeling it into constructive learning experiences, teachers often expend energy subduing children's physicality. . . . What if, instead, teachers used kinesthetic language to teach elementary curricular subjects?" (1998, 1). Learning is not confined to our heads. Movement is learning, exploration, and investigation.

We are constantly "reading" and interpreting body language as part of how we communicate, but often this is not a skill that is developed intentionally. In addition to activating learning, students also benefit from developing their understanding of how they communicate using nonverbal language. Jessica Brownfeld argues that verbal language, which includes "speaking, listening, reading, and writing," is one way of communicating, but we also draw heavily on our ability to read and communicate in nonverbal language (2010). She adds, "Though each type of language can function effectively in their respective arenas, communication can occur on a deeper level if both communicative forms are used together" (2010, 8). Brownfeld advocates for education not only to connect to students' minds but to become an embodied process, that, quoting from Liz Lerman, "uses the body and the body's internal and external awarenesses as a partner in acquiring knowledge, assuaging curiosity, and pursuing being a human being" (Brownfeld 2010, 10).

> "Students who are given the opportunity to create art will create something that in some way reflects their own culture. If students see their culture reflected in the environment, and are given the space to express themselves through their art making, that will help to create that safe environment."
>
> —Deirdre Moore (2016, para. 18)

This chapter considers the possibilities for integrating creative movement across the curriculum to investigate curricular topics.

What Is Creative Movement?

In creative movement, students make choices about how they will use their bodies to express ideas and concepts. In the classroom, creative movement can be applied to curriculum material students are studying. From the solar system to mathematical equations to a journey on a steamship coming to the United States to the transformation of caterpillars to butterflies, creative movement has applications across curriculum and grade levels. As such, it is a powerful tool for connecting curriculum concepts to personal expression and experience, providing a rich and unforgettable educational experience for students. It does not require pretraining in movement or a particular physical ability. Creative movement draws from the innate human ability to communicate through movement (Miller and Glover 2010).

You might be wondering, *What's the difference between movement in drama (pantomime) and creative movement?* Creative movement is more abstract than movement in drama. The focus is on the movement itself, not on pretending to move like an animal, plant, or character. Sandra Minton notes that creating movement pieces "involves connecting movements together to produce short pieces of movement or sequences, and ultimately shaping these sequences" (2003, 39).

Creative movement is not about learning "steps" or "moves." It is "about using the thinking tools of dance to create and build analogical and metaphoric connections between embodied experience and curriculum content. These interpretations are at once expressive and intellectual, individual and collaborative" (Celeste Miller, pers. comm.).

Why Does Creative Movement Matter?

"Self-awareness and self-management are fundamentally rooted in the body, making dance an excellent tool for building such competencies as emotional awareness, accurate self-perception, and impulse control."

—Margot Toppen (2019, para. 7)

Like other forms of artistic exploration, creative movement can be used as an inventive approach to investigate specific curricular content, express understanding, and explore ideas. Creative movement "also connects us to our body and this connection, often ignored, allows us to investigate intuitive honing and to begin to understand ourselves in relationship to ideas" (Bartholomew, pers. comm.). This form of embodied learning is how many students learn best.

The Mind–Body Connection

Bringing movement into the curriculum will benefit all learners by engaging their entire system for learning. "Movement awakens and activates many of our mental capacities. Movement integrates and anchors new information and experience into our neural networks, and movement is vital to all the actions by which we embody and express our learning, our understanding, and ourselves" (Hannaford 2005, 107).

Too often learning is treated as a "disembodied process" (Hannaford 2005, 15). Claudia Cornett notes that students benefit from integrating brain and body, because when the body is engaged, more parts of the brain are activated (2003). Eric Jensen confirms this connection between mind and body, saying that movement can "activate far more brain areas than traditional seatwork" (2001, 72). Griss elaborates, "Watch a group of healthy children at play. No doubt they will be moving. Even without hearing their words you will probably know what's going on by watching their activity, their body language, their physical energy dynamics. Children use their bodies to play, communicate, and express emotions" (1998, 1).

Brain researchers are discovering that incorporated movement and other senses are solidifying learning by supporting the development of neural pathways (Zull 2002). Biologist Carla Hannaford describes the way left and right brain functions can work together through movement. She says, "The logic hemisphere (usually the left hemisphere) tends to deal with details, the parts and processes of language and linear patterns. By contrast, the gestalt (usually the right hemisphere)—meaning whole processing or global as compared to linear—tends to deal with images, rhythm, emotion, and intuition" (2005, 90). The goal is to have the hemispheres work together in integrated thinking. She goes on to say that "the more we access both hemispheres, the more intelligently we are able to function" (Hannaford 2005, 91). Movement, then, can "anchor thought and build the skills with which we express our knowledge" (Hannaford 2005, 17).

The brain is constantly creating and connecting neural pathways. This neural plasticity allows the brain to learn and relearn. Hannaford discusses "the role of movement and play in activating" neural pathways, noting that there is a deep connection between body and mind that can enhance these neural pathways (2005). She says, "Movement activates the neural wiring throughout the body, making the whole body the instrument of learning" (2005, 18). Movement creates sensory experience, which builds neural networks.

Increasingly, studies show the impact on learning that movement and embodied learning can have. Using movement to physicalize curricular content has been linked to motivation (Fife 2003), improved science learning outcomes (Kreiser and Hairston 2007; Corbitt and Carpenter 2006; Plummer 2008), and improved math outcomes (Nemirovsky and Rasmussen 2005; Beaudoin and Johnston 2011).

Kinesthetic Learning

All of us are familiar with students who have a hard time sitting still—who learn best by moving and doing. These students are kinesthetic learners. Their primary mode of learning is through physical exploration and expression. Howard Gardner, in his book *Frames of Mind*, said that students who are strong kinesthetic learners have "the ability to use one's body in highly differentiated and skilled ways, for expressive as well as goal-directed purposes" (1983, 206).

In the Classroom

Celeste Miller, a teaching artist, choreographer, co-founder of Jacob's Pillow Curriculum in Motion®, and Lesley University adjunct faculty member, tells the story of one student in a kindergarten class who was learning about constellations: "The teacher had the kids sitting in a circle and she asked them to close their eyes. They sat there, faces scrunched, imagining. The teacher asked the students to visualize their favorite constellation. And students were working hard on this. Matthew begins to move around. The teacher asks him to come sit by her. Then she says to the group 'see the points of the constellation' in their mind's eye. And Matthew keeps getting up and placing his body in these different configurations. The class was videotaped. When the teacher watches the videotape later she realizes that Matthew wasn't squirming. He was forming the constellations with his body."

Often, students like Matthew struggle in the traditional classroom setting, where the primary instructional method involves passive sitting and listening. This traditional mode focuses on linguistic thinking and doesn't address students who learn better through visual, spatial, pattern, or conceptual thinking. Kinesthetic students make sense of the world through a series of complex nonlinguistic thinking functions. If we teach only to those who are strong in linguistic intelligence, we are not meeting the needs of all learners. In fact, all students can learn from engaging their bodies in learning. To truly meet the needs of all our diverse learners, we must incorporate varied approaches in our teaching, including the ability to explore ideas through movement.

Education, for the most part, is designed to support linguistic approaches to learning. Not everyone processes information in the same way. The body has knowledge of its own. Ever play an instrument and realize that you forgot the song but your fingers remember how to play? Physical memory is an important facet of learning. Researchers have found that learners acquire and store knowledge in two primary ways: *linguistically* (by reading or hearing lectures) and *nonlinguistically* (through visual imagery, kinesthetic, or whole-body modes). The more students use both systems of representing knowledge, the better they are able to think about and recall what they have learned (Marzano, Pickering, and Pollock 2001). "Not only does the body gather sensory information from the environment and send it to the brain, but it is also a site of knowledge construction and transmission" (Brownfeld 2010, 7).

Creative Movement and Higher-Order Thinking Skills

> *"We only believe those thoughts which have been conceived not in the brain but in the whole body."*
>
> —W. B. Yeats

The processes triggered by working with the brain and body in conjunction deepen cognitive development in the categories that the new Bloom's Taxonomy identifies as significant: creating, evaluating, analyzing, applying, understanding, and remembering (Anderson 2012). This is what Robert and Michele Root-Bernstein termed "body thinking" (1999). The concept is that embodying ideas is a way of thinking. Don't we want to give our students every way we can to construct meaning and express ideas?

Integrating movement across the curriculum works students' conceptual abilities, which is one area of higher-order thinking where students often struggle. Students work with curricular content as raw material and physically express their understanding and knowledge of the content in their own creative movement (Miller and Glover 2010a). In the creative process of making a movement representation of the concepts, students engage higher-order thinking skills. They also edit and refine as they go. They practice divergent thinking as they try out several ideas to choose the one that best expresses the concept. And they work collaboratively.

In the Classroom

Celeste Miller and J. R. Glover give an example of a student working on an exploration of *All Quiet on the Western Front* by Erich Maria Remarque (1929). One student was walking to portray a soldier. "We used walk because soldiers walk! Soldiers don't twirl!" (referring to another group who had used "twirling" as their enter/exit movement choice). The artist pushed students' thinking beyond making literal connections, noting, "In a literal interpretation of the text, you will find no twirling soldiers in the book. However, a soldier's thoughts might twirl. Their heart might twirl. Perhaps their world twirls. The changing landscape might appear to twirl. And so on. This is how we can encourage our students into the realm of abstract and metaphorical thinking." The artist then shifted instructions to spark ideas in a new direction by noting, "In our work we won't be 'soldiers' but we will perhaps be their thoughts, their moods, their hopes or fears. As you make your movement choices, think about how the protagonist's thoughts move—are they heavy, burdened, spinning, recoiling? What is the change in the 'verbs' of how his thoughts can be described as moving?" Miller noted, "In creative movement we can look to movement as a way to get to thematic, conceptual, metaphoric, and symbolic analysis of the text."

Creative movement provides a unique opportunity to develop students' abstract-thinking capacity, their ability to think conceptually and critically. Minton suggests that "concepts can be translated into movement by producing an abstraction of the original concept" (2003, 37). By this she means that the "essence of an idea can suggest or hint at the real thing, rather than looking like the real thing" (Minton 2003).

Abstract Thinking through Movement

Integrating creative movement into your curriculum is an opportunity to examine particular qualities, themes, patterns, and ideas rather than tell a story as you might in drama. For example, in a second-grade classroom, we might ask students to show something that is solid with their bodies. Students are asked to brainstorm words as they explore ideas through shape and movement. How might you show liquid with your body? As students describe the words that come to mind as they embody the ideas of solids and liquids, you can note the emerging list of descriptors—*splatter, splash, flow, trickle, stream, puddle*. Find the movement quality for each and consider the differences. What's the difference between a trickle as opposed to rushing? Students translate these ideas back and forth between movement and words. You could provide some gentle coaching to guide them and encourage exploration in movement, saying, for example, "Imagine you are a quick-moving stream. Show me with your body how the water flows, its jumps, its curves." Students use those great critical-thinking skills. They're asked to come up with movement, and they want to make the movement qualities rich, while they're expanding an entire list of descriptive words that capture the qualities of water. Suddenly they are choreographers creating movement phrases that capture the qualities of the liquid (Celeste Miller, pers. comm.).

The ideas are actively constructed; it's experiential, and it's reflective, evolving, collaborative, and problem solving. You can ask students to use movement to find the essence of the ideas they are exploring. There are endless ways to put together movement in effort, space, and time. Students can layer in story, memory, and literal things as well as more abstract ideas. The elements of movement provide a huge palette that is at students' fingertips as they physicalize ideas. There are so many aspects of movement to explore and experiment with—ideas such as repetition, exaggeration, tempo, and order. Students use their bodies to express and explore. They make choices about how they move in space and time to express ideas. By bringing movement into the classroom, we expand the repertoire for learning, assessment, and sharing knowledge and understanding (Celeste Miller, pers. comm.).

In the Classroom

Keri Cook, a fourth-grade teacher in Georgia, describes watching how students moved easily into the concept of seasons through creative movement. She says, "As I watched them craft their seasons (through creative movement activity), they needed very little input from me. It was what came natural to them. I watched them spin, and turn, and tilt, and revolve, and become unified. There was not a second of boy/girl cooties at any point. They weren't boys and girls . . . they were the sun, they were the earth, they were the wind, they were leaves on trees, swimming pool covers, snowmen . . . they were fantastic. . . . And they were moving . . . and they got it! No book, no paper, just them and their bodies."

Creative movement works as metaphor. George Lakoff and Mark Johnson describes metaphors as containers for meaning (2003). They speak of metaphor in terms of linguistic expression, but in fact, movement creates visual and embodied metaphors. Metaphors not only make our thoughts more vivid and interesting; they actually structure our perceptions and understanding. Metaphor is exploring one idea through the frame of another. Working through movement allows us to journey into the content and explore it in new ways. "As students learn the creative movement elements of body, energy, space, and time, they also learn how to analyze and categorize their thinking" (Cornett 2003, 293).

Divergent Thinking

Ken Robinson, in his TED Talk "Ken Robinson Says Schools Kill Creativity" (2006), makes the case for needing a learning revolution to change the paradigm on traditional forms of teaching. He notes that most learning is from the head up. This is a loss. He says, "I think math is very important, but so is dance. Children dance all the time if they're allowed to; we all do. . . . Truthfully what happens is, as children grow up we start to educate them progressively from the waist up. And then we focus on their heads. And slightly to one side."

We want our students to have creative capacity. Divergent thinking is a necessary skill for this kind of approach. Robinson defines *divergent thinking* as "being able to identify lots of possible answers to a question—to move beyond thinking in linear ways or convergently" (2010). By engaging in an aesthetic experience through the arts, Robinson says, your senses are operating at their peak. He notes a study that shows how children are naturally divergent thinkers, scoring at genius level in kindergarten, and how they lose this ability as they get older. Interestingly enough, creativity is lost as they become "educated." Robinson advocates for education that is less about conformity and more about allowing students to develop their unique talents and creativity. Can we imagine education differently by broadening our repertoire of teaching strategies to meet the needs of all students and support their connection to and engagement with the curriculum?

For some students, this way of knowing is critical. When students reflect on moments where movement connects them to their ideas, the case for movement in the classroom becomes compelling: "Dance allowed me to express myself without talking," and "I've always been better at nonverbal communication" (Jacob's Pillow Dance Festival 2010). Where would these students have been without access to movement? When information is translated into new forms such as dance, students draw upon their prior knowledge and experiences, and unique interpretations are the result. Brownfeld discusses the connection between mind and body and, drawing from John Bulwer's research, notes that in some cases, "the body can make discoveries the mind cannot" (Brownfeld 2010, 24).

Standards

Creative Movement in the College and Career Readiness Standards

Creative movement helps students develop higher-order thinking skills by translating text and speech to the symbolic language of movement and back again. As they respond to text through movement, students can make logical inferences, determine central ideas or themes, analyze how events and ideas develop over the course of a text, interpret words and phrases, and integrate and evaluate content, all of which are included in the standards.

Getting Started with Creative Movement

"In order to problem solve through dance, the most effective way to do that is to not first think but to first do. And so this requires a great deal of being able to listen to oneself, to trust oneself, and to take and intuit even when you don't really understand what you're doing. You need to first begin moving your body and allow your body to come up with some ideas. You have to go back to the mental to sort out, to edit yourself, to select out of those initial ideas what has the strongest connection, resonance with you, but first you've just got to jump in there and do something."

—Jack Bartholemew, physics teacher (2010)

Warm-Ups

Using movement to warm up the body and mind can provide the immense benefits of increased oxygen flow, blood circulation, and glucose production (Jensen 2001). Movement warm-ups can be used to get the class focused, as a break to get back on task, or for a transition into a new topic. As the student physicalizes an idea, the brain forms new ways to make associations with the material being presented, creating stronger neural pathways (Zull 2002). Warm-ups, such as asking students to move in different ways; using movements that are sharp, curvy, straight, choppy, and so on; and noticing how movement qualities communicate differently are key to building skills and using movement in a safe, constructive, community-supportive, peer-supportive way before we even go there at all.

The B.E.S.T. System

Creative movement is a form of dance and as such utilizes the elements universal to all dance, including body, energy, space, and time (B.E.S.T.). In creative movement, understanding the basic elements of dance and the vocabulary of movement provides a place to begin looking at or "reading" movement and dance. Dance is an abstract art form, and rather than telling a story, it can reveal patterns, spatial designs, conceptual ideas, and emotions. Creative movement can add depth to the ways students investigate and know and how they express and explore meaning. When students are provided with basic vocabulary, they can describe what they notice and how they make their choices in developing work. Share the B.E.S.T. system with students so they can access this important vocabulary.

- **B—Body** is the instrument of dance. A variety of shapes and moves can be created using the body. Movement can be done with the body as a whole unit or with isolated parts (hips, legs, feet, hands).

- **E—Energy** (or Effort) is the choice of *how* to move the body. A walk sped up becomes a run. A casual walk changes when knees are lifted high, with more force, and it turns into a march. Arms can curve soft circles through the space or move sharply to resemble the motion of a robot. Emotions can be suggested depending on how a movement is performed. A run can suggest freedom or fear depending on how the energy is used and directed during the run.

- **S—Space** is where movement takes place and where it moves to and from. It can be explored by making the body big or small or moving on different levels. Movement can travel through space in different directions (forward, backward, sideways, diagonal) and use different pathways (straight, curved, circular, zigzag). Movements that travel through space are called *locomotor*. Examples of common locomotor movements are walking, skipping, running, and galloping. Movements done while rooted to one spot are called *axial* (think of Earth spinning on its axis). Examples of axial movements are twisting, bending, and reaching.

- **T—Time** addresses how long a movement lasts and how it is measured. Movement can be measured by counts, flavored with rhythm, or even timed to an internal, intuitive sense of how long something lasts without counts or beats. Movement can be slowed down or sped up. Movement can explore acceleration and deceleration as well as a variety of rhythms.

Every movement choice students make and execute uses the elements of dance. Paying attention to the elements makes movement choices and observations richer. For example, the sentence *The girl ran* can be much more interesting using the elements of dance: *The little girl lifted her knees high and threw her head back as she bounded quickly across the room to greet her father.*

Overcoming Discomfort

Understanding our own discomfort in trying something new is part of the learning curve for incorporating new teaching strategies. It takes courage to try out new ways of teaching. It requires courage on the part of the teacher and students to try new ways of learning. A sedentary class will have a mixed response when movement is added. Some students will be joyous; others will be nervous. The nervousness caused by the newness might cause resistance and other symptoms of discomfort. We must face our own discomfort as well—our discomfort with moving, our discomfort moving with others, our discomfort trying something new. There are societal pressures as well. At the high school level, students worry about their "coolness" and how they will be seen (Miller and Glover 2010a, 7). Still, the benefits far exceed the sense of discomfort that comes with taking risks.

Introductory Activity: Movement Strings

Celeste Miller proposes a scaffolding process for using creative movement that can be broken down into four steps. This process can be accomplished in a 20- to 60-minute learning block, depending on the classroom situation, and will engage students in using creative movement as a tool for learning. The process begins by brainstorming a list of descriptive and action words about the unit of study. These words will become the source for the students' movements. Then, students work in small groups to create *movement strings* (sometimes known as *movement phrases*) that express the curricular ideas. This is followed by reflection and assessment.

1. **Brainstorm:** Brainstorm with students movement words and ideas related to a curricular topic. Develop a vocabulary word and phrase list from the brainstorm and display it in the classroom. This list can be used to increase student vocabulary in general, deepen curriculum topic knowledge, and serve as a source for the students' movement-making choices.

2. **Develop movement strings:** Have students work in small groups to build their movement strings. Tell them to choose words and phrases from the brainstormed list, then select and arrange physical movements into a movement string (or phrase) that expresses those ideas. Introduce students to the elements of dance—body, energy, space, and time (B.E.S.T.)—with a brief introduction, chart, or illustration. Tell students to use B.E.S.T. to enhance their movement choices.

3. **Share:** Have students share their movement strings with their classmates. Ask the audience to use observational comments to talk about both the creative movement choices and the content connections. Ask questions to draw out learning moments

in both what viewers notice and what each group learned as they developed their work.

4. **Assess:** Have students discuss or write about the process of creating movement strings, focusing on how their knowledge of curricular content changed. Create a rating scale or rubric to formally assess both the curricular content and the movement skills shown in students' movement strings.

Creative Movement across the Curriculum

Creative movement, working with B.E.S.T., can "convey an idea, message, or emotion just as a writer would use written language to combine words and sentences into an essay or other composition" (Brownfeld 2010, 25). Engaging in the creation of creative movement work and dance as well as "viewing dance are ways to transmit nonverbal knowledge" (Brownfeld 2010, 25). Moving between written and verbal language and nonverbal language can support the development of each. Brownfeld notes, "Where one language falls short, the other can compensate" (2010, 26). And she continues, "A body's actions have the ability to communicate at the same level as words . . . however at times the body's ability to transmit messages can surpass that of words" (2010, 28). In short, developing both verbal and nonverbal languages can strengthen communication. In the examples that follow, you will see how education can be strengthened by using "active, or embodied learning as opposed to passive learning methods, such as drilling and memorization" (Brownfeld 2010, 38).

Creative Movement in Language Arts

When students translate text into movement, they draw on higher-level thinking skills. Use creative movement to explore literary terms and plot lines, including exposition, setting, characters, rising action/complications, climax, falling action, and resolution/denouement from different stories. Have students work together in small groups to create a movement string (or phrase) (a plan for a movement phrase) exploring the use of levels and movement across space to represent their understanding. Then have them perform their pieces to show what they have learned. Incorporate creative movement into vocabulary work by having students create movements inspired by new words.

In the Classroom

A high school class read *The Maltese Falcon* by Dashiell Hammett, and students were asked to identify the various, often conflicting, personality traits of the main character, Sam Spade. In small groups, students selected one character trait—corrupt, ethical, amorous, or existential, for example—and with paper and markers, drew a visual map of the trait's development over the course of the novel. The following steps became the means for the teacher to evoke deeply meaningful discussions as well as finely articulated written assignments from the students about the novel's complexities.

Classroom teacher Mike Mooney worked with choreographer and Jacob's Pillow Curriculum in Motion® artist-educator Nicole Livieratos and students to investigate the visual character maps as reflections of the written tone and imagery in the story. Students were asked, "How might you represent what is happening physically?" They responded by translating their maps into set spatial pathways. Next they found a section of Hammett's text that described the character trait they were working with and used it as inspiration to create movements that traveled along the spatial pathway.

Students created visual representations of Sam Spade's path of corruption, which they represented through movement.

Mooney and Livieratos routinely shifted student attention from working on their movement studies to pausing for a discussion about the process. This enabled students to deeply tap into the gestures, behavioral patterns, energy, images, and movement styles of archetypes found in the novel, which further enhanced their movement studies. As a result, students connected to their inner feelings and experiences to create a traveling movement phrase full of rich variations in timing, rhythm, pacing, levels of the body in space, dynamics, tension, suspense, and surprising twists. Whether crawling, rolling, twirling, folding, or furling, the entire class was able to witness how character traits give shape and definition to actions and decisions made along the pathway of a novel or one's life.

High school students presenting their movement string documenting the character pathways of Sam Spade. (Jacob's Pillow Curriculum in Motion® residency)

Creative Movement in Social Studies

Use movement to explore the personal experiences of people throughout history; for example, have students embody the emotions of immigrating to the United States coming through Ellis Island or create a movement phrase with symbolic movement to show aspects of a period, such as the Civil War. Students could create short creative movement pieces about the forces at work during World War II or the range of emotions triggered by a government policy. "A dance of anger can be explosive . . . it can be passive anger twisting in on itself and being still and quiet" (Priscilla Harmel, pers. comm.).

Have students use movement to represent processes, such as how an ear of corn makes its way from a farmer's field to a bowl of cornflakes (Peggy Barnes, pers. comm.) or how mail makes its way from one address to another. Have them create a flow chart and bring the process to life through movement.

When working with creative movement, ask students questions such as "What makes it less literal? What are more abstract ways to convey an idea? What happens if you make it much bigger, or much smaller? How might you play with transitions? How can you use this particular art form to express line and shape?" (Priscilla Harmel, pers. comm.).

Creative Movement in Mathematics

Ask younger students to develop choreographed movement phrases that include number patterns (for example, 3 rows of dancers performing 4 spins each = 12 spins). Then have students share their movement pieces with classmates who identify the patterns being presented (Griss 1998). Ask students to embody geometric shapes. This can be done using their bodies or using giant elastic bands to stretch into a variety of shapes showing dimensionality. Students can create and describe patterns visually and through gesture. Have students enact mathematical problems physically, such as: *Eight birds are sitting on a telephone wire—three fly away. How many birds are left on the wire?* (Priscilla Harmel, pers. comm.).

Have older students demonstrate solving one- and two-step equations using creative movement, making connections between mathematical ideas and symbols. Begin with equations that reflect two equal expressions. To keep the equations balanced, whatever students do on one side of the equal sign, they must also do on the other side.

Creative Movement in Science

Physicalizing scientific concepts and processes helps students internalize and truly understand. Have students show through movement the shifting of the tectonic plates of Earth and the forces at work: the oozing lava and the building pressure of magma. Ask students: "How do different plates move in relation to each other (convergent boundaries, divergent boundaries)? How does the movement of the plates trigger earthquakes, volcanic activity, mountain-building, and oceanic trench formation along these plate boundaries?" Students will discover ideas and identify questions that need to be researched as they translate ideas from texts into movement. You can ask students: "What do these words mean? How will you convey those meanings through physicalization?" (Priscilla Harmel, pers. comm.)

Students also can use movement to show ecological shifts from unique perspectives. For example, ask students to create a movement piece that examines the threat of extinction of a particular species of fish, in which they imagine the struggle of the fish. By embodying it, they come to understand the animal and the concept of extinction in a different way.

Use movement to explore processes of many kinds. Have students work through the water cycle by first moving through the vocabulary and then embodying each phase of the cycle in movement. Ask them to imagine the force of the rain falling to the earth. How might they represent the flow of the rain coming down through their bodies? As the water dries up and evaporates, it would be a different, lighter kind of movement. Students must think about how their movement can use different qualities to portray the change in the water as it moves through the cycle. There are many scientific processes that lend themselves to this kind of physical embodiment (Priscilla Harmel, pers. comm.).

Creative movement is well suited to showing action of any kind. Ask students to show in movement the timing of a particular process, how quickly a chemical reaction might move, or how sound moves through different materials. To create a movement piece, students will need to research the qualities they want to convey and make them visible through movement (Priscilla Harmel, pers. comm.).

In the Classroom

A third-grade class at the Silvio O. Conte Community School in Pittsfield, Massachusetts, culminated a Jacob's Pillow Curriculum in Motion® residency by demonstrating to the second grade what they learned about states of matter. First, the students showed solid, liquid, and gaseous states in their bodies by using moments of stillness, moving through space fluidly, and embodying the frenetic activity of molecules heated into steam. Next the students brought these movement ideas together and physically expressed how solid transforms to liquid (melting), how liquid changes to gas (evaporation), how gas becomes liquid (condensation), and how liquid turns to solid (freezing). The creative ways in which students chose to transition between states of matter formed a captivating, artistically shaped movement phrase, and at the same time, revealed how clearly the students understood the scientific processes taking place at the molecular level behind the vocabulary (Jacob's Pillow Curriculum in Motion® 2012).

Rita Walden's second-grade class in Aiken, South Carolina, created a "butterfly dance" in which they moved through the phases of transformation from caterpillar to butterfly.

From caterpillar eggs, to chrysalis . . .

. . . to emerging butterfly, to flight.

Note how much is conveyed by shape and movement about what students understand about the development process. Considering the results of her arts-integrated work with students, Walden reflects, "These lessons were fun, hands-on, interesting, fact-filled ways to learn more about the butterfly. I found my students to be excited to take risks without worrying about failing. . . .They found their unique way of applying the knowledge they had to the activities. . . . I firmly believe that the hands-on approach using the arts allows a passion to come alive in students."

You can see what students have learned by the way they translate ideas into physical form. For informal, on-the-spot assessment, ask students to answer you in movement; tell them, "Show me with your body." If you are teaching about different sources of energy, ask students to show you what happens if something is heated or cooled, or if you are working on statistics, ask students to show you their understanding of *mean, median, mode,* and *outlier.* Sometimes students who have difficulty expressing their understanding verbally or in written form will surprise you with what they know. Identifying what students have learned through movement can then provide a sense of next steps for sharing that knowledge in text-based ways as well.

In the Classroom

One teacher who tried movement in the classroom for the first time pointed out one little boy and said, "You know, I've had so much trouble with him all year because I'm not sure he's getting it. And there's a bit of a language barrier. But I watched him and every time he was asked to show his understanding in movement, I could see how deeply he understands this material because he had so many answers for me in movement."

Concluding Thoughts

"Figuring out things in your body and through movement weaves ideas together. This builds a sense of intuitive knowledge, of working with an interchange of acting and responding, of physical problem solving."

—Paula Aarons, former classroom teacher and
Jacobs Pillow Curriculum in Motion® artist-educator

Paula Aarons, former classroom teacher and Jacobs Pillow Curriculum in Motion® artist-educator notes, "When we ask students to begin moving, we find heart rate going up, changes in breathing patterns, tactile senses begin to come alive, physical senses start to operate on a higher frequency. . . . These are real physiological things that happen." She notes that integrating creative movement provides new pathways for learning. This physical problem solving allows students to "do first and think later as a way to generate ideas, explore concepts in new ways, draw out knowledge, and analyze through a sensory approach" (Paula Aarons, pers. comm.). As a result, ideas are solidified and descriptive language is developed side-by-side with the movement exploration.

Aarons adds, "As educators we must remember that knowledge is not contained just in words. Intuitive knowledge matters—there is a value of experiencing feeling and feelings in the body. The content we explore in classrooms is often rational, definable, and tangible. But intuition, a felt sense of things, has an important place in learning as well" (Paula Aarons, pers. comm.).

As Nancy King writes in her book *Giving Form to Feeling*, dance (creative movement) "is surely a most extraordinary fusion of thinking, doing, and feeling. If we are concerned about the health of a child's mind, body, and spirit, then how can we ignore the education force of an art form which addresses all three at once?" (1975). We want students to become active learners. "What better way to engage them in mastering curriculum than allowing them to physically embody big ideas and nuanced knowledge through their bodies?" (Miller and Glover 2010b).

Reflection

1. Thinking about your current curriculum, what opportunities do you see where movement can play a role in exploring abstract ideas or concepts?

2. What might diverse learners gain by "doing first and thinking later"?

3. How might you use movement to help students in curricular problem solving?

Chapter 7

Planning
and
Assessment

Planning and Assessment

A New Lens for Planning and Assessment

In designing arts-integrated instruction, teachers plan with standards or clear objectives in mind, then select strategies and create instructional activities that align with meeting these goals. Assessment is an important aspect of planning to provide feedback along the teaching and learning process for both teachers and students that they are on track to meet their projected outcomes. Planning with assessment in mind ensures that a full picture of student learning emerges throughout the learning process. Formative assessment through documentation and assessment tools helps both student and teacher see where they have been and where they are going and allows them to adjust their teaching and learning processes to best achieve the stated goals. Summative assessment provides a complete picture of not only what students know but how they understand curricular content.

Literally translated, *assessment* means "to sit beside." This invites the idea of a dialogue about learning that happens between teacher and student. Gail Burnaford, Arthur Aprill, and Cynthia Weiss equate assessment with research, drawing from the idea that "re/search—[meaning] to look again [is] . . . a process of inquiry, questioning, and looking for something" (2001, 90). Seen in this light, assessment becomes a collaborative inquiry between teacher and student investigating the teaching and learning process. Looking at arts-based processes and products can provide rich details that reveal not just *that* students know but *how* they know (Goldberg 1992).

In this chapter, we explore strategies for making assessment a core aspect of the teaching and learning process, identifying questions to explore about the learning process with students, collecting a variety of learning evidence, analyzing what the data tell us, and thinking carefully about how to tell the story of learning. Assessment drives planning and instruction in a feedback loop that moves students forward in the learning process.

Using the example of an arts-integrated lesson on Faith Ringgold's *Tar Beach* (see the full plan in Appendix A), this chapter will illustrate each step of planning and implementing an arts-integrated unit. The Unit Planning Chart in Appendix B shows the unit goals and standards, the teaching strategies, the assessment tools that will be used, and the evidence and documentation that will be collected. In Appendix C, a blank unit planning chart is provided for your use.

Unit Planning: Mapping Lesson Plans through the Evidence Chart

The evidence chart in Figure 7.1, from *Teacher as Curator: Formative Assessment and Arts-Based Strategies* (Donovan and Anderberg 2020), is a helpful planning tool for mapping the evidence you will collect to document that students have met the standards for arts and non-arts content. By unpacking standards into specific, documentable evidence of learning and identifying strategies to collect evidence of learning, your plan will align closely to your original goals. See the *Tar Beach Unit Outline* in Appendix A (page 194) and the *Unit Planning Chart* in Appendix B (page 198) for a detailed example.

Figure 7.1 Teacher as Curator: Evidence Chart Template

Standards	Specific Evidence of Learning Targets (Assessment Criteria)	Collection Strategies (Formative Assessment and Summative Tasks)
Arts standard(s): Select arts standards that will work well to deepen learning in an integrated lesson or unit.	Detail what students will know and be able to do: Consider varied evidence that allows students to demonstrate understanding of the subject area. • What criteria should be considered as you collect evidence? • What will you look for in the evidence? • What can be documented? • What will students be able to demonstrate?	How will you collect evidence? (Methods can include arts-based approaches.) Consider varied methods for collecting evidence that include arts-based approaches allowing students to demonstrate understanding.

Figure 7.1 Teacher as Curator: Evidence Chart Template *(cont.)*

Non-arts standard(s): Select non-arts standards that will work well to deepen learning in an integrated lesson or unit.	Detail what students will know and be able to do. Consider varied evidence that allows students to demonstrate understanding of the subject area.	How will you collect evidence? (Methods can include arts-based approaches.) Consider varied methods for collecting evidence that include arts-based approaches allowing students to demonstrate understanding.
	• What criteria should be considered as you collect evidence?	
	• What will you look for in the evidence?	
	• What can be documented?	
	• What will students be able to demonstrate?	

Source: Donovan and Anderberg (2020)

To ensure true arts integration, plan your lesson or unit intentionally to make sure you are doing the following:

- teaching with equal rigor about arts as well as non-arts content
- assessing learning in both arts and non-arts content
- using the arts as a strategy to assess learning

The evidence chart will help in planning for strong arts integration. In the *Tar Beach Unit Outline* (Appendix A), you will see that drama, visual arts, and social studies standards were selected; evidence of learning for each standard was identified; and then the instruction strategies for collecting evidence of learning are detailed (close observation of the image, performance of a devised theater piece, and the creation of a story quilt). The evidence chart not only aligns instruction with evidence of learning and standards but also creates a map for the lesson plan or unit.

Elements of Artistic Literacy

A key area to include in the development of your unit plan (and in your evidence chart planning process) is the vocabulary of the art form. Asking students to learn and use the vocabulary of an art form is important for developing artistic literacy. Once students understand the language of an art form, they can more accurately discuss artistic choices they make in their own work, as well as what they notice in the work of others. Understanding the elements of an art form and how they can be used in different ways leads to craft.

There are varied ideas about elements of the arts in the field. After careful consideration, we've documented ideas we feel are valuable to fostering arts integration.

Visual Art

The elements of visual art were informed by a review of the field, including the J. Paul Getty Museum (Getty, n.d.-a), the Institute for Arts Integration and STEAM (Riley 2017), and the Kennedy Center (Glatstein 2019).

Line: A mark made by the path of a point moving in space; lines can be horizontal, vertical, or diagonal; they can vary in width, direction, and length.

Shape: A closed line; shapes can be geometric, often made up of straight edges, or they can be organic and made up of irregular, free-form edges; shapes are flat and can be a defined by length and width.

Color: The response of the eyes to different wavelengths of light reflecting off objects; color can be defined by any of its three properties: hue (or name, such as red, blue, or green), intensity, and value.

Form: A three-dimensional shape that can be expressed by length, width, and depth.

Texture: The quality of a surface that can be seen and felt (rough, smooth, bumpy, and so on); texture can be real or implied, meaning that a surface can have a physical texture or visually appear to have a texture even though the surface is flat.

Value: The lightness or darkness of a color.

Space: The area between, around, above, below, or within objects; space can be defined as negative (such as the emptiness of holes) or positive; space also describes depth, or the illusion (idea) of depth.

Principles of Design

These are informed by the J. Paul Getty Museum (Getty, n.d.-b), the Institute for Arts Integration and STEAM (Riley 2017), the Kennedy Center (Glatstein 2019), and PBS Learning Media (KET, 2014).

Balance: Arrangement of art elements with attention to visual weight. Symmetrically balanced artworks feel stable; asymmetrically balanced artworks can create a feeling of instability or movement.

Movement: An artwork can be composed suggesting a sense of action. The elements of art can be intentionally placed in ways that guide the viewer's eyes around the work.

Repetition: Applying art elements so that the same element(s) are used again and again; repeating elements in a predictable way creates pattern.

Proportion: Size relationship between objects or elements in an artwork.

Emphasis: The part of the artwork that stands out in an eye-catching way; the center of interest.

Contrast: The juxtaposition of elements in an artwork showing differences that make them stand out from each other; many things can be in contrast to each other, including colors, shapes, or textures.

Unity: The use of elements of art to create harmony in a composition.

Variety: Combining art elements in ways to create visual interest.

Storytelling

There are five key elements to storytelling (National Storytelling Network, n.d.). To learn more about these elements, visit **storynet.org/what-is-storytelling/**.

Interaction: The storyteller actively engages the audience and adapts based on the energy and response of the audience. As a result, every time the story is told it changes.

Words: The storyteller uses words (spoken, signed, or manual) to create connections and invite listeners into the story world through sensory details.

Actions: The story is activated through vocalization, physical movement, and small and large gestures.

Story: The storyteller shares a narrative that has characters and action.

Imagination: Storytellers encourage the active imagination of the listeners.

Music

According to Jacobsen (1992) and Estrella (2019), these are the basic elements of music from a Western perspective.

Pitch: The highness and lowness on a musical scale.

Harmony: Notes of different pitches played at the same time.

Melody: How notes are put together in a sequence.

Dynamics: The loudness and quietness of composition (musical piece) and transitions between the two.

Rhythm: How time is controlled in music (beat, meter, tempo).

Timbre/Tone Color: The sound quality of a note.

Texture: The number of layers in a composition (musical piece).

Drama

These definitions are adapted from a variety of sources, including the "Drama Handbook" (International School of Athens, n.d.), "The 12 Dramatic Elements" (Cash, n.d.), and "Elements of Drama" (Windmill Theatre Company, n.d.).

Roles: The characters (people, animals, objects, ideas, and more) in a drama.

Tension: Dramatic friction or opposition that emerges from a conflict, struggle, or juxtaposition of ideas or motivations; dramatic tension drives action and generates interest.

Time: The pacing of how action moves as the drama unfolds.

Dialogue: The words spoken by characters in a drama.

Situations: The circumstances that frame the drama and identify what is happening and what the problem is.

Space: Where the drama unfolds or the use of the performance space; also the positioning of the body across levels in space (low, medium, and high).

Creative Movement

These elements are drawn from several sources, including the Kennedy Center (Bodensteiner 2019), PBS Learning Media (KQED 2015), the Institute for Arts Integration and STEAM (Riley 2017), the National Core Arts Standards, and the Perpich Center for Arts Education (2009).

Body: Creative movement works with the parts of the body to move, isolate, manipulate to create shape and movement through space.

Space: Creative movement interacts with and occupies space on different levels, in different pathways, in different size and scope of movement.

Action: *Non-locomotor*, which is axial movement around the body's axis and *locomotor*, movement that travels through space.

Time: Movement happens over time and can communicate through tempo and rhythm.

Energy: The qualities (sustained, percussive, suspended, etc.), weight (heavy, light, etc.), and flow (continuous, controlled, etc.) of how movement occurs.

Poetry

The following list of terms related to poetry is informed by the Academy of American Poets (n.d.), and the work of Kwame Alexander (2019), Georgia Heard (1999), and Mary Oliver (1994).

Sound: The creation of meaning with sound, often through the use of onomatopoeia, assonance, consonance, alliteration, and more.

Rhythm: The beat of the poem, created through pattern, repetition, rhyme, syllables, and more.

Imagery: Precise word choices and figurative language create an image in the reader's mind by evoking the senses and imagination.

Structure: The organization of ideas. Some poems are free verse, others follow a specific form. Intentional line breaks and use of space on the page create meaning.

Density: What is said (or can be said) in the space; density distinguishes poetry from regular speech and prose.

Audience: Poets write with their audience in mind, revealing tone or attitude toward the message, subject, and more.

Curator Lens in Lesson Planning

Donovan and Anderberg, in their book *Teacher as Curator: Formative Assessment and Arts Based Strategies*, invite educators to think of themselves through the lens of a curator: "Finding synergies between the content you select and the entryways for learning is an art. The standards help drive deeper understandings, but it takes orchestration of the many elements to create learning opportunities that are seasoned with a mix of resources, pedagogies, and curriculum. Beyond searching for content online or by other means, content curation involves organization of content. It often involves putting content into categories or themes" (2020, 45). In other words, lesson design is a creative process, and thinking about your role as a curator is a reminder that every choice you make as an educator makes a difference.

Documentation: Plan to Gather Evidence

"When teachers document their work, they create an archive of learning that can inform their methodologies. They learn from their investigations and from the work that their students produce. Critical observations during documentation can reveal evidence of learning and help you improve your own classroom practice" (Donovan and Anderberg 2020, 182).

Once curricular goals, standards, arts-integrated activities, and strategies have been selected, plan how to document the process of learning. Documentation provides students with information about their progress toward meeting learning goals (formative assessment) and provides a clear picture at the end of the learning process of what students have attained (summative assessment). There are opportunities for assessing learning through students' artistic work. Collecting the right evidence reveals not just that students know but how they know (Goldberg 1992), because documentation provides a wider frame than traditional assessment. Often work takes place in a learning situation, but it is not documented well or ends up being considered a display at the end of the learning process. Documentation provides a critical feedback loop that links the objectives students set out to meet and the outcomes at which they arrive.

At the beginning of a unit, plan how to document the work well through the teaching and learning process to ensure that there is evidence to draw on, showing that students have met the unit learning goals. Plan to collect certain types of documentation with the objectives in mind. But as additional, unexpected learning is revealed through the arts, document evidence of that learning as well. In arts-based work, teachers never can predict every result and are often happily surprised at the ideas that come forward from students' investigations. These in-process moments help show connections students make along the way.

Collect documentation in individual student portfolios that are available for both student and teacher to access at any time. If you are ready with a camera and sticky notes during student work time, you will find it easy to take quick photos or jot observations and place them in student portfolios at the end of the day. Also, get students in the habit of placing work samples and other evidence of learning in their portfolios. They often will surprise you with their insights into their own learning processes.

Documentation and evidence of student learning can include the following:

- student work samples (sketches, notes, scripts, images, storyboards, and so on)
- photos or videos of student work processes
- transcripts or videos of discussions and debriefings
- student journals or learning logs
- teacher observation notes
- interviews (audio or transcript)
- exit slips
- written peer or self-critiques
- assessment tools: checklists, rating scales, rubrics, and note-taking tools

Documentation of Formative Assessment

"Collecting evidence of learning throughout the learning process provides ongoing feedback about teaching and learning, what's working and what needs to be tweaked. Formative assessment can keep you focused on all that evidence conveys about what is unfolding, about your process, about the learning and needs of documentation, reflection, and creative work" (Donovan and Anderberg, 2020, 182).

Assessment should be situated at the juncture between teaching and learning, becoming a central part of the learning process. As researchers at Project Zero, an educational research group at Harvard University, notes, "Assessment does not have to be a post-mortem. In the United States, when we think about documentation, we typically have more of a record-keeping than a learning mentality" (Project Zero 2006). Formative assessment is defined by Paul Black and Jane Jones as providing "information to be used as feedback, by teachers, and by their pupils in assessing themselves and each other, to modify the teaching and learning activities in which they are engaged" throughout the process of learning (2006). This means that formative assessment strategies are ongoing throughout the process of learning, providing teachers with information about where they need to go next with their teaching and providing students with ongoing feedback.

In arts-integrated learning this means looking at what is discovered in the creative process as students discuss their creative choices and reflect on how they have translated ideas into new forms. Thinking together throughout the learning journey allows both student and teacher to course-correct as needed. As teachers see how students are accessing content and expressing their understanding, they can adjust their teaching to provide the right next step for students as they learn. Larry Ferlazzo notes, "When students are asked to think about what they have learned and how they have learned it (the learning strategies they've used), they are better able to understand their own learning processes and can set new goals for themselves" (2012).

This back-and-forth progression is made easier with documentation to draw from. As students show their work through sketches, notes, scripts, videos, images, audiotapes, and other documentation and share ideas through discussions and debriefing, learning logs and journals, and conferencing, they can self-assess, work with peers for feedback, and conference with teachers for a clear picture of where they are in achieving objectives and what they need to do next to deepen their learning.

In the *Tar Beach* unit, formative and summative assessment documentation could include the following:

- note-taking tool completed by teacher during observation of the performance
- list of brainstormed words and ideas used by students in creation of their piece
- documentation of discussions held
- photographs/videos of in-process development of the performance
- rubric/observation sheet completed by actors, peers, and teacher critiquing in-process sharing of devised work
- documentation of the process of developing story quilts and written narratives
- discussion of artistic choices

Documentation in Summative Assessment

Summative assessment evaluates what has been learned at the end of the process. In addition to traditional paper-and-pencil testing, look at the entire learning process through the documentation that has been collected in student portfolios. Judy Arter and Vicki Spandel describes the portfolio as "a purposeful collection of student work that tells the story of the student's efforts, progress, or achievement in (a) given area(s). This collection must include student participation in selection of portfolio content, the guidelines for selection, the criteria for judging merit, and evidence of student self-reflection" (1991).

Portfolios allow teachers to do the following:

- collaborate with students to document a more detailed picture of student learning
- include evidence of learning that occurs throughout the creative process, not just a cumulative product at the end

- track how students arrive at an answer (this can be as important as the answer itself)
- use authentic approaches to work that mirror real-life contexts

Students should be equal partners in the process of creating and reflecting on the work collected to tell the story of their learning. Students can be at the center of telling their own stories, helping to document processes, select work samples, collect reflections, and organize materials in a thoughtful way that communicates well.

Portfolios can be used to review progress with students and parents. Looking together at a wide range of evidence can lead to reflective conversations that are useful for both teachers and students. Portfolios also provide evidence of how well students have achieved goals, benchmarks, and standards for determining grades.

For the *Tar Beach* unit, final summative assessment, assembled in student portfolios, includes the following:

- teacher notes on observations made during formative assessments
- photographs of the final tableaux
- teacher and student rating scales on final tableaux

Exhibition

Showing student work in an exhibition or public performance can provide strong summative evidence of how students work with curricular ideas as they translate content into artistic work that reveals understanding. Sharing the work with an outside audience can do the following:

- provide opportunities for students to record their learning process
- allow for critique, which is a natural outgrowth of the process of art-making and can prompt reflection and discussion both on a personal level and in peer-to-peer critique as students comment on one another's work
- give a visual documentation of students' progress
- provide time and space for review and discussion of work

Assessment Tools

In addition to documenting student work through the collection of evidence, plan to create and use note-taking tools, checklists, rating scales, and rubrics to formally evaluate how the evidence shows students' attainment of learning goals. These assessment tools should be used not only by teachers but also for peer feedback and student self-critique during the creative process. All these tools can be used in both formative and summative evaluation, but each tool provides a different level of detail and specificity. As part of unit planning, create assessment tools and decide when and how they will be used. Collect completed assessment tools in student portfolios as part of an overall picture of student learning.

Note-Taking Tools

The simplest assessment tool focuses on observation without requiring evaluation or rating. Create a note-taking chart, such as the one shown in Figure 7.2, or a simple list of questions to guide observation of student work and provide focus on specific standards and goals. A note-taking tool completed by a teacher or peers can provide valuable formative feedback to students during the creative process, as well as describe evidence of student learning at the end of a unit of study. Design your observation questions to draw out evidence of learning linked to your standards (and evidence identified in your chart).

Figure 7.2 Note-Taking Tool for Devised Theater Performance

Group Name *or* Students in Group	
How did the students bring their response to, and observation of, the illustration to life using elements of drama?	
What curricular content (social studies, visual art, theater) was evident in the performance?	
How did the students' explanation of their group process reveal curricular understanding?	

Checklists

Arnold Aprill, founder and former creative director of Chicago Arts Partnerships in Education (CAPE), notes that checklists help teachers see "the simple presence or absence of characteristics, actions, and qualities" (2011). There is no evaluation made of the work; a checklist simply shows what is and is not present. Figure 7.3 shows a checklist used in the *Tar Beach* unit.

Figure 7.3 *Tar Beach*: Checklist of Expectations for Story Quilts

Students have done the following:

- shown understanding of the role of illustration in activism
- used source material (artwork) to inform their responses
- depicted ideas in visual and narrative forms to create a compelling story quilt
- articulated their interpretation of how images can affect change
- analyzed and explained personal preferences and constructed meaning through visual responses in story quilts

As formative assessment, checklists can be used as a quick measure of whether students are on track and what they need to add to their work. Checklists also can be used as summative assessment to show that students have met the requirements of an assignment or project. Checklists can note the inclusion of both content-area and arts components.

Rating Scales

A rating scale can show how students have demonstrated learning goals on a continuum. For each learning goal or assignment requirement, respondents choose a statement or number to indicate students' level of attainment of that goal or requirement. This is one step beyond a checklist, showing not only whether students have included required components but how well they have addressed the requirements. A rating sheet is not as thorough as a rubric and does not take as long to complete, providing a quick way to give students feedback on their work. Figure 7.4 shows an example of a rating scale.

Figure 7.4 *Tar Beach* Devised Theater Performance Rating Scale

How Effectively Have Students . . .	1–5	Notes
Devised theater that uses the elements of drama in effective ways		
Demonstrated in their dramatic choices or in discussion evidence of key ideas from Ringgold's art		
Demonstrated use of brainstormed responses to the illustration compiled from the group		
Shown an understanding of the role of illustration in activism		

As formative evaluation, rating sheets tell students where they are in the process of addressing requirements and where they need to do more work. They can be used as teacher-, peer-, or self-critique. As summative evaluation, rating sheets show evaluation of completed work measured against standards and goals.

Rubrics

Rubrics, like rating scales, evaluate performance characteristics on levels, indicating the degree to which a standard or requirement has been met. But unlike a rating scale, a rubric includes specific descriptions of each rating, telling exactly how students' work addresses learning goals.

Teacher-created rubrics should be available to students at the beginning of the learning process so they can see specifically what they are expected to do or show. Whenever possible, involve students in creating rubrics to increase investment in and ownership of the process and provide students with an opportunity to think about learning from an outcomes perspective. Learning is deepened when teachers and students collaborate on setting expectations and reviewing the evidence of learning together.

As formative assessment, rubrics provide specific, detailed descriptions for students of how their work will be measured. Rubrics can be used for both peer feedback and student self-critique so that students can evaluate their own work and revise as necessary. As summative assessment, rubrics show in detail how students have demonstrated their understanding and to what extent they have attained standards and learning goals. Rubrics should address both content-area and arts standards and goals. The rubric in Figure 7.5 is for summative evaluation of the *Tar Beach* performance.

Figure 7.5 *Tar Beach* Devised Theater Performance Rubric with Space for Notes

Assessment Criteria	Proficient	Developing	Not Yet
Examines Ringgold's art to determine key themes			
Brainstorms descriptive and observational language derived from the art			
Uses words and phrases from the brainstormed word bank to create a devised theater piece			
Creates a compelling performance including tableau, words, and movement			
Explains artistic choices using the vocabulary of drama			

A Complete Picture of Learning

At the end of a unit of instruction, student portfolios provide a complete picture of student learning, showing both what they know and how they came to know it. Through documentation gathered during the learning process and completed assessment tools, a true picture emerges of each student's achievements. Have students share their portfolios with their families. Portfolios provide evidence that teaching through the arts not only addresses standards but takes students on an in-depth journey of learning.

Concluding Thoughts

We hear increasingly about data-driven decision making. The need to collect evidence and use it to inform decisions makes sense, particularly in understanding what students have learned, how they have learned, what teaching has been effective for student learning, and where improvement is needed. Unfortunately, the data are too often drawn from a narrow focus on content knowledge and skill. The arts can provide a layered look at students' learning. There are many aspects of learning and expression taking place in the creative process, and mindful, well-constructed documentation can make these learning strands visible and honor the complexity of teaching and learning.

Writer Natalie Goldberg notes that by writing about our experiences, "we live our life twice" (1998). In other words, we can reflect on and explore what has happened to us and the choices we have made and notice the specifics of what we have been involved with and how we have made meaning of it. This is true of the process of documentation as well. If we engage our students in the documentation process, asking them to think about how to put together traces of learning in ways that tell the story of learning, they will learn about their own processes and how their choices affect their learning. In addition, we will gain valuable insight about our teaching choices and learning and about what we value, as well as assess how we have met the objectives of our curriculum.

Teachers who integrate the arts often describe the results as transformative—for them and for the way they see student learning. The arts provide flexible ways for students to represent their understanding. Taking the time to collect and share evidence of this understanding can help teachers and students reveal the layers of learning that occur in this type of work. Students who are provided with artistic avenues for expressing understanding and sharing their ideas in different symbolic systems or languages can bring forward individual voice and perspective. Taken together, using all the languages available to us, this type of assessment provides a more holistic and human view of learners. We can tell their stories in all their complexity.

Reflection

1. What are some advantages of documenting the creative process of learning?

2. How might careful documentation expand on the use of assessment tools?

3. What benefits do students gain by reviewing documentation alongside teachers?

References Cited

Academy of American Poets. n.d. "Glossary of Poetic Terms." Accessed October 1, 2021. poets.org/glossary.

Adichie, Chimamanda. 2016. "The Danger of a Single Story." maorilandfilm.co.nz/chimamanda-ngozi-adichie-the-danger-of-a-single-story.

Aguirre, Lidia. 2020. "Choosing Culturally Responsive Images to Connect with Students." *Edutopia*, October 14, 2020. www.edutopia.org/article/choosing-culturally-responsive-images-connect-students.

Alexander, Kwame. 2019. *The Write Thing: Kwame Alexander Engages Students in Writing Workshop and You Can Too!* Huntington Beach, CA: Shell Education.

American Association of School Administrators. n.d. "Life Ready." *National College and Career Readiness Indicators*. Accessed August 13, 2021. www.redefiningready.org/life-ready.

Anderson, Lorin. 2012. "Bloom's Taxonomy, New Version." Old Dominion University. www.odu.edu/educ/roverbau/Bloom/blooms_taxonomy.htm.

Aprill, Arnold. 2011. "What Do We Measure How?" Chicago Arts Partnerships in Education, Arts Assessment Toolbox.

Arter, Judy, and Vicki Spandel. 1991. *Using Portfolios of Student Work in Instruction and Assessment*. Portland, OR: Northwest Regional Educational Laboratory.

Atwell, Nancie. 1998. *In the Middle*. Portsmouth, NH: Heinemann Press.

Banks, James A. 1994. *An Introduction to Multicultural Education*. Boston: Allyn and Bacon.

Bataineh, Ruba Fahmi, and Na'em Ali Salah. 2017. "The Effectiveness of Drama-Based Instruction in Jordanian EFL Students' Writing Performance." *TESOL International Journal* 12 (2): 103–118.

Beach, Richard, Deborah Appleman, Susan Hynds, and Jeffrey Wilhelm. 2002. *Teaching Literature to Adolescents*. New York: Lawrence Erlbaum.

Beaudoin, Colleen, and Pattie Johnston. 2011. "The Impact of Purposeful Movement in Algebra Instruction." *Education* 132 (1): 82–96.

Bellisario, Kerrie, Lisa Donovan, and Monica Prendergast. 2011. *Promising Pathways: Studies on Arts Integration*. Cambridge, MA: Lesley University.

———. 2012. *Voices from the Field: Investigating Teachers' Perspectives on the Relevance of Arts Integration in Their Classrooms*. Cambridge, MA: Lesley University.

Bensusen, Sally J. 2020. "The Power of Observation: Practical Art-Based Exercises to Improve How We Learn Science." *Science and Children*. 57 (5). www.nsta.org/science-and-children/science-and-children-january-2020/power-observation

Birge, Edward Bailey. 1984. *History of Public School Music in the United States*. Boston: Oliver Ditson Company.

Black, Paul, and Jane Jones. 2006. "Formative Assessment and the Learning and Teaching of MFL: Sharing the Learning Road Map with the Learners." *Language Learning Journal* 34 (1): 4–9.

Blanco, Richard. 2017. "Video: A Teacher's Guide to Poets.org." Poetry Foundation. poets.org/text/video-teachers-guide-poetsorg.

Boal, Augusto. 1995. *The Rainbow of Desire: The Boal Method of Theater and Therapy*. New York: Routledge.

———. 2002. *Games for Actors and Non-Actors*. London: Routledge.

Bodensteiner, Kirsten. 2019. "Do You Wanna Dance? Understanding the Five Elements of Dance." The Kennedy Center. www.kennedy-center.org/education/resources-for-educators/classroom-resources/media-and-interactives/media/dance/do-you-wanna-dance/.

Booth, Eric. 1999. *The Everyday Work of Art: Awakening the Extraordinary in Your Daily Life*. Naperville, IL: Sourcebooks.

Bradby, Marie. 2000. *Mama, Where Are You From?* New York: Orchard Books.

BrainyQuote. n.d. "Elton John Quotes." www.brainyquote.com/authors/elton-john-quotes.

Brooks, Katherine. 2017. "'Migration is Beautiful' Documentary: Artist Favianna Rodriguez Talks Immigrant's Rights and Arts' Role in Politics." *Huffington Post*. December 6, 2017. www.huffpost.com/entry/migration-is-beautiful-artist-favianna-rodriguez-documentary_n_2535690?ncid=edlinkusaolp00000003/.

Brownfeld, Jessica Marie. 2010. "The Dancing Classroom: Bringing the Body into Education through the Creative Process." Bachelor of Arts thesis, Wesleyan University.

Burdette, Martha. 2011. "Arts Integration: The Authentic Context for 21st Century Learning." The Southeast Center for Arts Integration. centerforartsintegration.org/articles/arts-integration.

Burnaford, Gail, Arnold Aprill, and Cynthia Weiss. 2001. *Renaissance in the Classroom: Arts Integration and Meaningful Learning*. Mahwah, NJ: Lawrence Erlbaum.

Carr, Margaret. 2001. *Assessment in Early Childhood Settings: Learning Stories*. Thousand Oaks, CA: SAGE.

Cash, Justin. n.d. "The 12 Dramatic Elements." *The Drama Teacher* (blog). Accessed October 1, 2021. thedramateacher.com/wp-content/uploads/2008/02/The-12-Dramatic-Elements.pdf.

Center for Applied Special Technology (CAST). n.d. "About Universal Design for Learning." Accessed October 1, 2021. www.cast.org/impact/universal-design-for-learning-udl/.

Christensen, Linda. 2001. "Where I'm From: Inviting Students' Lives into the Classroom." *Rethinking Our Classrooms* 2: 22–23.

Common Core State Standards Initiative. 2010. *Common Core State Standards*. Washington, DC: National Governors Association Center for Best Practices and the Council of Chief State School Officers. www.corestandards.org.

Corbitt, Cynthia, and Molly Carpenter. 2006. "The Nervous System Game." *Science and Children* 43 (6): 26–29.

Cornett, Claudia. 2003. *Creating Meaning through Literature and the Arts: An Integration Resource for Classroom Teachers*. 2nd ed. Upper Saddle River, NJ: Pearson.

Costello, Rachel. 2019. "The Benefits of Storytelling: Help Kids Develop Social Emotional Learning." Yo Re Me Kids. www.yoremikids.com/news/storytelling-benefits-child-development.

Creegan-Quinquis, Maureen, and Joan Thormann. 2017. "Effective Use of Technologies to Transform Arts Education and Teach Diverse Learners." In *Art and Technology: The Practice and Influence of Art and Technology in Education*, edited by Luisa Menano and Patricia Fidalgo. Rotterdam, the Netherlands: SensePublishers.

DBI Network. n.d. "Guided Imagery." The University of Texas at Austin. dbp.theatredance. utexas.edu/content/guided-imagery.

Dessen, Sarah. 2008. *Just Listen.* New York: Penguin.

Dewey, John. 1931. *Philosophy and Civilization.* New York: Minton.

Diaz, Gene, Lisa Donovan, and Lousie Pascale. 2006. "Integrated Teaching through the Arts." Presentation given at the UNESCO World Conference on Arts Education, Lisbon, Portugal, March 8, 2006.

Diaz, Gene, and Martha Barry McKenna, eds. 2017. *Preparing Educators for Arts Integration: Placing Creativity at the Center of Learning.* New York: Teachers College Press.

Doherty, Timothy J. 1996. "College Writing and the Resources of Theatre." Unpublished dissertation, University of Massachusetts.

Donovan, Lisa. 2005. "The Aesthetics of Listening: Creating Spaces for Learning." Doctoral dissertation, Lesley University.

Donovan, Lisa, and Sarah Anderberg. 2020. *Teacher as Curator: Formative Assessment and Arts-Based Strategies.* New York: Teachers College Press.

Donovan, Lisa, Richard Shreefter, and Marianne Adams. 2005. *Curriculum Resource Guide: A Sharing of Arts Based Strategies for Learning.* Cambridge, MA: Creative Arts in Learning Division at Lesley University National Arts & Learning Collaborative (NALC). www.artslearning.org/files/NEACurriculumResourceGuide. pdf.

Dooley, Roger. 2010. "Stories Synchronize Brains." *Neuromarketing: Where Brain Science and Marketing Meet.* www.neurosciencemarketing.com/blog/articles/stories-synchronize-brains.htm.

Dudding, Kate. 2005. "The Value of Storytelling in Education." www.katedudding.com/value-storytelling-education.htm.

Dunleavy, Jodene, and Penny Milton. 2008. "Student Engagement for Effective Teaching and Deep Learning." *Education Canada* 48 (5): 4–8.

Estrella, Espie. 2019. "An Introduction to the Elements of Music." *LiveAbout*. November 4, 2019. www.liveabout.com/the-elements-of-music-2455913.

Ferlazzo, Larry. 2012. "Response: Ways to Include Students in the Formative Assessment Process." *Classroom Q&A with Larry Ferlazzo (EducationWeek blog)*, January 10, 2012. blogs.edweek.org/teachers/classroom_qa_with_larry_ferlazzo/2012/01/matt_ townsley_asked_carol_boston.html.

Fife, Britiney Michelle. 2003. "A Study of First Grade Children and Their Recall Memory When Using Active Learning in Mathematics." Master's thesis, Johnson Bible College.

Fishman-Weaver, Kathryn. 2019. "How Creating Visual Art Contributes to SEL." *Edutopia*. April, 29, 2019. www.edutopia.org/article/how-creating-visual-art-contributes-sel?fbclid =lwAR1ueBthSGTt17bnb5pz8UiDaXlxUFDHFX1qFgcjKNH2H6KMqdommk7vvNUw

Fletcher, Jill. 2018. "The Value of Teaching Contemporary Poetry." *Edutopia*, October 9, 2018. www.edutopia.org/article/value-teaching-contemporary-poetry.

Forsyth, Nicole. 2015. "Tell Me a Story: The Power of Narratives in Social and Emotional Learning (SEL)." *SEEN*, April 17, 2015. www.seenmagazine.us/Articles/Article-Detail/ articleid/4664/tell-me-a-story-the-power-of-narratives-in-social-and-emotional- learning-sel.

Frye, Elizabeth M., Woodrow Trathen, and Bob Schlagal. 2010. "Extending Acrostic Poetry into Content Learning: a Scaffolding Framework." *The Reading Teacher* 63 (7): 591–595.

Gallas, Karen. 1991. "Art As Epistemology: Enabling Children to Know What They Know." *Harvard Educational Review* 61 (1): 40–51.

Gardner, Howard E. 1983. *Frames of Mind: The Theory of Multiple Intelligences*. New York: Basic Books.

Gere, Jeff, Beth-Ann Kozlovich, and Daniel A. Kelin, II. 2002. *By Word of Mouth: A Storytelling Guide for the Classroom*. Honolulu, HI: Pacific Resources for Education and Learning.

Gill, Sharon Ruth. 2007. "The Forgotten Genre of Children's Poetry." *The Reading Teacher* 60 (7): 622–625.

Glatstein, Jeremy. 2019. "Formal Visual Analysis: The Elements and Principles of Composition." The Kennedy Center. www.kennedy-center.org/education/resources-for-educators/classroom-resources/articles-and-how-tos/articles/educators/formal-visual-analysis-the-elements-and-principles-of-compositon/.

Goldberg, Merryl. 2012. *Arts Integration: Teaching Subject Matter Through the Arts in Multicultural Settings*. 4th ed. Boston: Pearson.

Goldberg, Merryl R. 1992. "Expressing and Assessing Understanding Through the Arts." *Phi Delta Kappan*. 73 (8): 619.

Goldberg, Merryl, and Ann Phillips, eds. 1995. "Arts as Education." *Harvard Educational Review* 24.

Goldberg, Natalie. 1998. *Writing Down the Bones: Freeing the Writer Within*. Boston: Shambhala.

Goral, Mary Barr, and Cindy Meyers Gnadinger. 2006. "Using Storytelling to Teach Mathematics Concepts." *Australian Primary Mathematics* 11 (1): 4–8.

Gordon, John. 2009. "Sounds Right: Pupils Responses to Heard Poetry and the Revised National Curriculum for English." *The Curriculum Journal* 20 (2): 161–175.

Greene, Maxine. 1978. *Landscapes of Learning*. New York: Teachers College Press.

———. 1992. "The Passion of Pluralism: Multiculturalism and the Expanding Community." *Journal of Negro Education* 61 (3): 250–261.

Griss, Susan. 1998. *Minds in Motion*. Portsmouth, NH: Heinemann.

Grove, Robin, Catherine Stevens, and Shirley McKechnie. 2005. *Thinking in Four Dimensions: Creativity and Cognition in Contemporary Dance*. Carlton, Victoria, Australia: Melbourne University Press.

Hamilton, Martha, and Mitch Weiss. 2005. *Children Tell Stories: Teaching and Using Storytelling in the Classroom*. 2nd ed. New York: Richard C. Owen.

Hammett, Dashiell. (1929) 1992. *The Maltese Falcon*. New York: Vintage Books.

Hannaford, Carla. 2005. *Smart Moves: Why Learning Is Not All in Your Head*. Salt Lake City, UT: Great River Books.

Harjo, Joy. 2019. "An Interview with Joy Harjo, U.S. Poet Laureate." poets.org/text/interview-joy-harjo-us-poet-laureate.

Harpaz, Beth J. 2009. "Preventing High School Dropouts Can Start in 4th Grade." *Missourian*, August 11 2009. www.columbiamissourian.com/stories/2009/08/12/preventing-hs-dropouts-can-start-4th-grade.

Heard, Georgia. 1999. *Awakening the Heart: Exploring Poetry in Elementary and Middle School*. Portsmouth, NH: Heinemann.

Heathcote, Dorothy, and Gavin Bolton. 1995. *Drama for Learning: Dorothy Heathcote's Mantle of the Expert Approach to Education*. Portsmouth, NH: Heinemann.

Hetland, Lois, Ellen Winner, Shirley Veenema, and Kimberly M. Sheridan. 2013. *Studio Thinking 2: The Real Benefits of Visual Arts Education*. New York: Teachers College Press.

Homann, Maria. 2017. "How Science Teachers Can Use Storytelling." www.labster.com/how-science-teachers-can-use-storytelling.

Hubbard, Ruth. 1987. "Transferring Images: Not Just Glued on the Page." *Young Children* 42 (2): 60–67.

iDevelop Teacher Training. 2019. "Using Drama in the Classroom." idevelopcourses.com/using-drama-classroom.

International School of Athens. n.d. "Drama Handbook." Accessed May 4, 2021. isa.edu.gr/files/319/Drama_Handbook.pdf.

Intrator, Sam M., and Megan Scribner. 2003. *Teaching with Fire: Poetry That Sustains the Courage to Teach*. San Francisco, CA: Jossey-Bass.

J. Paul Getty Museum. n.d.-a. "Elements of Art." Accessed October 1, 2021. www.getty.edu/education/teachers/building_lessons/formal_analysis.html/.

J. Paul Getty Museum. n.d.-b. "Principles of Design." Accessed October 1, 2021. www.getty.edu/education/teachers/building_lessons/formal_analysis2.html

Jacob's Pillow Dance Festival. 2010. "Choreographers Lab 2010: The School at Jacob's Pillow." www.youtube.com/watch?v=1LZHiHsKG7M.

Jacobsen, Daniel Christopher. 1992. *A Listener's Introduction to Music*. Dubuque, Iowa: Wm. C. Brown Publishers.

Janeczko, Paul B. 2011. *Reading Poetry in the Middle Grades: 20 Poems and Activities That Meet the Common Core Standards and Cultivate a Passion for Poetry.* Portsmouth, NH: Heinemann.

Jensen, Eric. 2001. *Arts with the Brain in Mind.* Alexandria, VA: Association for Supervision and Curriculum Development.

Johnson, Thomas H., ed. 1960. *The Complete Poems of Emily Dickinson.* Boston: Little, Brown and Company..

Juster, Norton. (1961) 1988. *The Phantom Tollbooth.* New York: Bullseye Books.

Kelin, Daniel A. 2020. "Cultivating Change by Integrating Drama: A Classroom Experience." artistsandclimatechange.com/2020/10/14/cultivating-change-by-integrating-drama-a-classroom-experience.

Kennedy, Randy. 2006. "Guggenheim Study Suggests Arts Education Benefits Literacy Skills." *New York Times*, July 27, 2006. www.nytimes.com/2006/07/27/books/27gugg.html.

KET. 2014. "Principles of Design." PBS Learning Media. pbslearningmedia.org/resource/459077ac-6d7d-4eef-bd7e-e38d12e7ce97/principals-of-design/

King, Nancy. 1975. *Giving Form to Feeling.* New York: Drama Book Specialists.

King, Nancy, and Jacy Ippolito. 2001. "The Stories Project: Storypartners in the Classroom." *The New Advocate* 14 (1): 69–79.

Koch, Kenneth. 1999. *Wishes, Lies, and Dreams: Teaching Children to Write Poetry.* New York: Harper Perennial.

———. 2012. "Rose, Where Did You Get That Red?" Poets.org. www.poets.org/viewmedia.php/prmMID/17152.

Koki, Stan. 1998. "Storytelling: The Hearts and Soul of Education." PREL Briefing Paper. Honolulu, HI: Pacific Resources for Education and Learning.

Korn, Randi. 2012. "Teaching Literacy Through Art." Solomon R Guggenheim Museum. www.guggenheim.org/images/lta/pdfs/Executive_Summary_and_Discussion.pdf.

Kozol, Jonathan. 2007. *Letters to a Young Teacher.* New York: Crown.

KQED Art School. 2015. "The Five Elements of Dance." PBS Learning Media. pbslearningmedia.org/resource/d7fcd19b-ee9b-4d90-a550-833fbe22865c/the-five-elements-of-dance/.

Kreiser, Brian, and Rosalina Hairston. 2007. "Dance of the Chromosomes: A Kinetic Leaning Approach to Mitosis and Meiosis." *Bioscene: Journal of College Biology Teaching* 55 (1): 6–10.

Ladson-Billings, Gloria. 1994. *The Dreamkeepers: Successful Teachers of African American Children.* San Francisco: Jossey-Bass.

Lakoff, George, and Mark Johnson. 2003. *Metaphors We Live By.* Chicago: University of Chicago Press.

Landrum, R. Eric, Karen Brakke, and Maureen A. McCarthy. 2019. "The Pedagogical Power of Storytelling." *Scholarship of Teaching and Learning in Psychology* 5 (3): 247–253. doi.org/10.1037/stl0000152.

Lansing, Kenneth. 2004. "Why We Need a Definition of Art." *Aristos: An Online Review of the Arts.* www.aristos.org/aris-04/lansing1.htm.

Lesh, Richard A., and Helen Doerr. 2003. *Beyond Constructivism: Models and Modeling Perspectives on Mathematics Problem Solving, Learning, and Teaching.* London: Routledge.

Lippert, Margaret. 2005. "Once Upon a Time, Long Ago: Finding and Adapting Folktales." In *Telling Stories to Children*, edited by Betty Lehrman, 37–40. Jonesborough, TN: National Storytelling Press.

Litz, Ron. 2020. "How to Use Art to Teach History." *Edutopia*, October 1, 2020. www.edutopia.org/article/how-use-art-teach-history.

Longfellow, Leanne. 2019. "Universal Design for Learning (UDL) and Differentiation." *Inclusive Education Planning*, June 3, 2019. inclusiveeducationplanning.com.au/uncategorized/universal-design-for-learning-udl-and-differentiation/.

Lopez, Jessica Helen. 2018. "Spoken Word Poetry as Medicine: A SEL Practice of Celebration and Identity for Indigenous and POC Youth." *Education First*, June 7, 2018. education-first.com/spoken-word-poetry-as-medicine-a-sel-practice-of-celebration-and-identity-for-indigenous-and-poc-youth.

Lovell, Taffy. 2008. "Diamante Poem." *Taffy's Writings*. taffyscandy.blogspot.com/2009/04/diamante-poem.html.

Lowell, Susan. 2000. *Cindy Ellen: A Wild Western Cinderella*. New York: HarperCollins.

Lown, Fredric, and Judith W. Steinbergh. 1996. *Reading and Writing Poetry with Teenagers*. Portland, ME: Walch.

Lynch, Maureen Ann. 2009. "Making the Relevant Connection: The Middle School Student and Poetry: An Understanding and Appreciation of Poetry to Inspire the Poet Within." Yale National Initiative. yale.edu/ynhti/nationalcurriculum/units/2005/1/05.01.03.x.html.

Lyon, George Ella. 2010. "Where I'm From." www.georgeellalyon.com/where.html.

MacDonald, Margaret Read. 1994. "Making Time for Stories." In *Tales as Tools: The Power of Story in the Classroom*, edited by Sheila Daley, 9–17. Jonesborough, TN: The National Storytelling Press, 1994.

———. 2006. *Tunjur! Tunjur! Tunjur! A Palestinian Folktale*. New York: Amazon Children's Publishing.

Marzano, Robert, Debra Pickering, and Jane Pollock. 2001. *Classroom Instruction that Works: Research-Based Strategies for Increasing Student Achievement*. Alexandria, VA: Association for Supervision and Curriculum Development.

Mathieson, Erica M. 2015. "The Impact of Creating Visual Arts on Reading Comprehension in Third Grade Students." *SOPHIA*. St. Catherine University. sophia.stkate.edu/maed/125/.

Mattson, Rachel. 2008. "Theater of the Assessed: Drama-Based Pedagogies in the History Classroom." *Radical History Review* 102: 99–110.

McCaslin, Nellie. 2000. *Creative Drama in the Classroom and Beyond*. White Plains, NY: Longman.

McIntosh, Peggy. 1990. *Interactive Phases of Curricular and Personal Revision with Regard to Race*. Wellesley, MA: Wellesley College Center for Research on Women.

McKim, Elizabeth, and Judith W. Steinbergh. 2004. *Beyond Words: Writing Poems with Children*. 3rd ed. Brookline, MA: Talking Stone Press.

Miller, Celeste, and J. R. Glover. 2010a. "Dancing with Our Textbooks on Our Heads. The Chronicles of Jacob's Pillow Curriculum In Motion® at Monument Mountain Regional High School Told Through Stories, Essays and Strategies for Dance as a Tool for Learning." Unpublished manuscript.

———. 2010b. "Unpacking the Kinesthetic Mode for Learning and Teaching: Jacob's Pillow Curriculum in Motion®." Research findings at Monument Mountain. Unpublished manuscript.

Minton, Sandra. 2003. "Using Movement to Teach Academics: An Outline for Success." *Journal of Physical Education, Recreation and Dance* 74 (2): 36–40.

Moore, Deirdre. 2016. "Culturally Responsive Teaching and the Arts." Institute for Arts Integration and STEAM. artsintegration.com/2016/07/13/culturally.

Morice, Dave. 1995. *The Adventures of Dr. Alphabet: 104 Unusual Ways to Write Poetry in the Classroom and the Community*. New York: Teachers and Writers Collaborative.

National Art Education Association. n.d. "National Visual Arts Standards." Accessed October 1, 2021. www.arteducators.org/learn-tools/national-visual-arts-standards/.

National Coalition for Core Arts Standards. 2014. "Glossary of Terms: Theatre." docplayer. net/29830664-Glossary-for-national-core-arts-theatre-standards.html.

National Storytelling Network. n.d. "What Is Storytelling?" Accessed April 30, 2021. storynet.org/what-is-storytelling/.

Nemirovsky, Ricardo, and Chris Rasmussen. 2005. "A Case Study of How Kinesthetic Experiences Can Participate in and Transfer to Work with Equations." Conference of the International Group for the Psychology of Mathematics Education (9–16), Melbourne, Australia.

New, David. 2009. *Listen*. National Film Board of Canada. www.nfb.ca/film/listen/.

New Zealand Ministry of Education. n.d. "UDL and Differentiation and How They Are Connected." *Te Kete Ipurangi* (TKI). Accessed August 13, 2021. www.inclusive.tki.org. nz/guides/universal-design-for-learning/udl-and-differentiation-and-how-they-are-connected.

Noddings, Nel. 2006. *Critical Lessons: What Our Schools Should Teach*. New York: Cambridge University Press.

Norfolk, Sherry. 2010. "Why Do Teachers Need to Learn About Storytelling?" Unpublished manuscript.

Norfolk, Sherry, and Jane Stenson. 2012. *Social Studies in the Storytelling Classroom: Exploring Our Cultural Voices and Perspectives*. Marion, Michigan: Parkhurst Brothers.

Nye, Naomi Shihab. 2011. "Naomi Shihab Nye on Inspiration." poets.org/text/video-naomi-shihab-nye-inspiration.

Oatley, Keith. 2008. "The Mind's Flight Simulator." *The Psychologist* 21: 1030–1032.

Odegaard, Marianne. 2003. "Dramatic Science: A Critical Review of Drama in Science Education." *Studies in Science Education* 39 (1) 75: 101.

Oliver, Mary, 1994. *A Poetry Handbook: A Prose Guide to Understanding and Writing Poetry*. Orlando, FL: Mariner Books.

O'Neill, Cecily. 1995. *Drama Worlds: A Framework for Process Drama*. Portsmouth, NH: Heinemann.

O'Neill, Cecily, and Alan Lambert. 1991. *Drama Structures: A Practical Handbook for Teachers*. Portsmouth, NH: Heinemann.

Page, Nick. 1995a. *Music as a Way of Knowing*. Portland, ME: Stenhouse.

———. 1995b. *Sing and Shine On*. Portsmouth, NH: Heinemann.

Parsons, Michael J., and H. Gene Blocker. 1993. *Aesthetics and Education: Disciplines in Art Education: Contexts of Understanding*. Urbana: University of Illinois Press.

Pascale, Louise. 2002. "Dispelling the Myth of the Non-Singer: Changing the Way Singing Is Perceived, Implemented, and Nurtured in the Classroom." Doctoral dissertation, Lesley University. ProQuest (ATT 3193398).

———. 2005. "Dispelling the Myth of the Non-Singer: Embracing Two Aesthetics for Singing." *Philosophy of Music Education Review* 13 (2): 165–175.

———. 2006. "Finding a Bucket to Carry the Tune: Ways to Shift the Paradigm For Non-Singing Classroom Teachers." *Massachusetts Music News* 40 (1).

Perfect, Kathy A. 1999. "Rhyme and Reason: Poetry from the Heart." *The Reading Teacher* 52 (7): 728–737.

Perpich Center for Arts Education. 2009. "The Elements of Dance." www.nationalartsstandards.org/sites/default/files/Dance_resources/ElementsOfDance_organizer.pdf.

Peterson, Elizabeth. 2018. "Teach SEAL While Listening to Music." *The Inspired Classroom*. theinspiredclassroom.com/2018/01/teach-sel-listening-music.

Pink, Daniel H. 2005. *A Whole New Mind*. New York: Riverhead Books.

Plummer, Julia. 2008. "Students' Development of Astronomy Concepts Across Time." *Astronomy Education Review* 7 (1): 139–148.

Poetry Foundation. n.d. "Biography: Kenneth Koch." www.poetryfoundation.org/bio/kenneth-koch.

Powell, Mary Clare. 1997. "The Arts and the Inner Lives of Teachers." *Phi Delta Kappan* 78 (6): 450–453.

Price, Lindsay. 2015. "Devising Exercises for the Drama Classroom." *Theatrefolk*. August 31, 2015. www.theatrefolk.com/blog/devising-exercises-for-the-drama-classroom/.

Project Zero. 2006. "Making Learning Visible: Understanding, Documenting, and Supporting Individual and Group Learning." Harvard Graduate School of Education. www.pz.harvard.edu/mlv/indexfd69.html.

Ranzau, Sara DuBose, and Thomas, Ashley. 2016. "Learning How to Use Drama in the Classroom: A Student Teacher's Journey." *English in Texas* 46 (1): 42–49.

Rasinski, Timothy. 2014. "Tapping the Power of Poetry." *Educational Leadership* 72 (3): 30–34.

Reeves, Douglas. 2009. "The Value of Culture." *Educational Leadership* 66 (7): 87–89.

Remarque, Erich Maria. 1929. *All Quiet on the Western Front*. Boston: Little, Brown and Company.

Rieg, Sue, and Kelli Paquette. 2009. "Using Drama and Movement to Enhance English Language Learners' Literacy Development." *Journal of Instructional Psychology* 36 (2): 148–154.

Riley, Susan. 2017. "The Elements of Art Anchor Charts." The Arts Integration Institute. artsintegration.com/2017/07/01/elements-art-anchor-charts.

Rinne, Luke, Emma Gregory, Julia Yarmolinskaya, and Mariale Hardiman. 2011. "Why Arts Integration Improves Long-Term Retention of Content. Mind, Brain, and Education." *Mind, Brain, and Education.* 5 (2): 89–96. doi.org/10.1111/j.1751-228X.2011.01114.x.

Ringgold, Faith. 1988. *Woman on a Bridge #1 of 5: Tar Beach.* Acrylic paint, canvas, printed fabric, ink, and thread, 189.5 × 174 cm. Guggenheim Museum Online Collection. www.guggenheim.org/artwork/3719.

Robinson, Ken. 2006. "Ken Robinson Says Schools Kill Creativity." TED Talk. www.ted.com/talks/lang/en/ken_robinson_says_schools_kill_creativity.html.

———. 2010. "Ken Robinson: Changing Education Paradigms." TED Talk. www.ted.com/talks/ken_robinson_changing_education_paradigms.html.

Root-Bernstein, Robert, and Michele Root-Bernstein. 1999. *Sparks of Genius: The Thirteen Thinking Tools of the World's Most Creative People.* Boston: Houghton-Mifflin.

Rosler, Brenda. 2008. "Process Drama in One Fifth-Grade Social Studies Class." *The Social Studies* 99 (6): 265–272.

Sabol, F. Robert. 2011. "The Importance of Providing Quality Art Education for All Students." *SEEN.* November 27, 2011. www.seenmagazine.us/Articles/Article-Detail/ArticleId/1818/The-importance-of-providing-quality-art-education-for-all-students/.

Schaefer-Simmern, Henry. 1950. *The Unfolding of Artistic Activity: Its Basis, Process and Implications.* Berkley, CA: University of California Press.

Schafer, R. Murray. 1992. *A Sound Education: 100 Exercises in Listening and Sound-making.* Indian River, Ontario, Canada: Arcana Editions.

Schutzman, Mady, and Jan Cohen-Cruz, eds. 1994. *Playing Boal: Theatre, Therapy, Activism.* New York: Routledge.

Shafak, Elif. 2010. *The Forty Rules of Love: A Novel of Rumi.* New York: Viking Adult.

Sheridan, Susan. 1997. *Drawing/Writing and the New Literacy.* Amherst, MA: Drawing/Writing Publications.

Showalter, Elaine. 2012. "Teaching Poetry." Blackwell. www.blackwellpublishing.com/Showalter/SampleChapters.htm.

Silverstein, Lynne B., and Sean Layne. 2010. "Defining Arts Integration." The John F. Kennedy Center for the Performing Arts. artsedge.kennedy-center.org/~/media/ArtsEdge/LessonPrintables/articles/arts-integration/DefiningArtsIntegration.pdf.

Sima, Judy. 2012. "Storytelling and Science—What a Concept." Michigan Association for Media in Education, Media Spectrum. www.judysima.com/pdfs/Storytelling%20and%20Science.pdf.

Slater, Jana Kay. 2002. "A Poet Came to Our Class." Poetry Evaluation Project, Executive Summary, California Poets in the Schools. www.cpits.org/background/evaluation_study/evaluation.htm.

Spector, Nancy. n.d. "Faith Ringgold: *Woman on a Bridge* #1 of 5: Tar Beach." Collection online, Guggenheim. Accessed August 20, 2021. www.guggenheim.org/artwork/3719.

Stenson, Jane, and Sherry Norfolk, eds. 2012. *Social Studies in the Storytelling Classroom: Exploring Our Cultural Voices and Perspectives*. Marion, MI: Parkhurst Brothers.

Stickling, Sara, Melissa Prasun, and Cora Olsen. 2011. "Poetry: What's the Sense in Teaching It?" *Illinois Reading Council Journal* 39 (3): 31–40.

Story Arts. 2000. "Why Storytelling?" *Storytelling in the Classroom*. www.storyarts.org/classroom/index.html.

Teitelbaum, Noah. 2021. "3 Tips to Turn Storytelling into a Social-Emotional Learning Activity." *Big Life Journal*, June 17, 2021. biglifejournal.com/blogs/blog/storytelling-social-emotional-learning-activity.

Tomlinson, Carol Ann. 2003. *Fulfilling the Promise of the Differentiated Classroom: Strategies and Tools for Responsive Teaching*. Alexandria, VA: Association for Supervision and Curriculum Development.

Toppen, Margot. 2019. "Using Dance to Promote SEL Skills." *Edutopia*, August 12, 2019. www.edutopia.org/article/using-dance-promote-sel-skills.

VanDerwater, Amy Ludwig. 2018. *Poems Are Teachers: How Studying Poetry Strengthens Writing in All Genres*. Portsmouth, NH: Heinemann.

Vincent. 2008. "Arctic." *In Our Write Minds* (blog), September 18, 2008. www.writeshop.com/blog/2008/09/18/diamante-contest-winners.

Whitin, David J. 1982. "Making Poetry Come Alive." *Language Arts* 60: 456–458.

Wilhelm, Jeffrey. 2007. *Language and Literacy: You Gotta BE the Book: Teaching Engaged and Reflective Reading with Adolescents*. New York: Teachers College Press.

Wilhelm, Jeffrey, and Brian Edmiston. 1998. *Imagining to Learn: Inquiry, Ethics, and Integration Through Drama*. Portsmouth, NH: Heinemann.

Willcox, Libba. 2017. "Vulnerability in the Art Room: Explorations of Visual Journals and Risks in the Creation of a Psychologically Safe Environment." *Art Education*. 70 (5): 11–19.

Windmill Theatre Company. n.d. "Elements of Drama." Accessed October 1, 2021. windmill.org.au/wp-content/uploads/2018/09/Elements-of-Drama.pdf.

Zemelman, Steven, Harvey Daniels, and Arthur Hyde. 1998. *Best Practice: New Standards for Teaching and Learning in America's Schools*. Portsmouth, NH: Heinemann.

Zull, James E. 2002. *The Art of Changing the Brain: Enriching the Practice of Teaching by Exploring the Biology of Learning*. Sterling, VA: Stylus.

Exploring Illustration through Faith Ringgold's *Tar Beach*

Essential Questions

Invite students to consider the following essential questions:

- What happens when theater artists use their imaginations and theater skills while engaging in creative exploration and inquiry? (from **www.nationalartsstandards.org**)

- How can we make sense of social narratives and history through viewing and responding to illustration art?

- How does knowing the contexts, histories, and traditions of art forms help us create works of art and design? Why do artists follow or break from established traditions? How do artists determine what resources and criteria are needed to formulate artistic investigations? (from **www.nationalartsstandards.org/sites/default/files/Visual%20 Arts%20at%20a%20Glance%20-%20new%20copyright%20info.pdf**)

Enduring Understandings

Students will understand:

- Dramatic exploration taps into intuition, imagination, and critical inquiry.

- Illustration art tells stories, shapes social and political narrative, and can create change.

- The arts translate ideas into new symbol systems and multimodal language.

The Invitation to Explore Illustration

Tell students they will spend time closely observing an image created by artist Faith Ringgold called *Tar Beach*. Ringgold first created a story quilt, then later re-created it as an illustration for the book *Tar Beach*. The image can be found at the Guggenheim Museum online (**www.guggenheim.org/artwork/3719**). Using the Visual Thinking Strategy approach (**vtshome.org**), engage students in a discussion about the image, drawing out as many insights and observations as possible using the following questions:

- What's going on in this picture?

- What do you see that makes you say that?

- What more can we find?

Ask participants to jot notes and descriptions documenting their observations phase of close looking during the discussion, noticing the way that the elements of visual arts (line, shape, color, form, texture, value, space) and principles of design (balance, movement, repetition/pattern, proportion, emphasis, contrast, unity, variety) are used to communicate meaning.

Discussion Questions

Reflect on the process by asking carefully crafted debriefing questions to draw out insights:

- How did the process of slow looking inform your analysis?
- What is Ringgold communicating with this image?
- How is symbolism used to communicate meaning?

Discuss with students what the list of words suggest about Tar Beach, and Ringgold's choices.

Introduce ideas about how illustration has been used by artists over time as a strategy for activism. According to Mary Berle, former Chief Educator of the Norman Rockwell Museum, "Illustration art is published imagery with a job to do." Berle notes:

- Illustration art tells a story. It reflects and shapes cultural narratives.
- Illustration art invites conversation, reflection and often action.
- Illustration art can teach about history; it is also helpful to understand historical context when making sense of images. Noticing what is missing in an image can be as important as noticing what is there.
- Illustrators, like all of us, continue to evolve as they are shaped by history and experience (pers. comm., July 2021).

Next, invite students to circle words and phrases of interest from the brainstormed list and use these words to craft several lines that distill the meaning they take away from deep engagement with this image. Invite participants to work in small groups to share what they wrote and integrate ideas to create a group poem or collage of ideas that can be performed. Explain that these ideas will be the raw material for a devised theater piece to be developed and shared with the class.

"Art is an important and perhaps unexpected tool in teaching history. Photos, drawings, and paintings can communicate an abundance of information about historical events. Students can analyze pieces of art to assist them in digging deeper into investigating an artist's perspective and decision making."

—Ron Litz (2020, para. 1)

Devised Theater Performance

Introduce the idea of devised theater as a collaborative creation using dramatic exploration without traditionally defined roles such as director or playwright. The creators are often also the performers and the "process of discovering the final product is as important as the final product itself" (Price 2015). Ask students to work in small groups to devise a dramatic performance of the collage of ideas that emerged during the writing phase.

Review the elements of drama (roles, tension, time, dialogue, situations, and space) and encourage groups to combine selected elements to make artistic choices. Ask them to include the following ingredients in their performance:

- use of tableaux—a still image at the beginning and end of their presentation
- performance of a devised theater piece using their voices to bring words to life
- a moment of movement
- a moment of choral speaking

Provide students with a copy of the rubric that will be used to evaluate their performance.

Have students share their in-process performance with the class and explain their thinking, artistic choices, key observations, and interpretation of the quilt. Debrief using the rubric and self and peer critiques. Students should use the feedback they receive to improve their work.

When students are satisfied with their work, create opportunities to share their performances. Save in-process artifacts and record student presentations for documentation. Complete the rubric for summative evaluation.

Designing a Story Quilt

Read the children's book *Tar Beach*. Ask students to discuss *Tar Beach* through the lens of activism.

- What is the story being told?
- What is the power dynamic that is reflected or shaped?
- What conversation does the art invite?

Introduce another illustration that explores a social or political theme, such as Yuko Shimizu's *Defend Democracy (Lady Liberty)* (2020). If this were a story quilt, what narrative might you add around the border?

Finally, invite students to generate ideas for a personal story quilt, including an image (selected or created) and a narrative around the border. Share the story quilt checklist (figure 7.3) for students to guide them as they plan their image.

Share images and discuss using these questions. Ask students to share their artistic and narrative choices using vocabulary of visual art (elements of visual art and principles of design).

- Write about a time when you experienced a power dynamic at play (personal experience, witnessed experience, book, image).
- How might you create an image (illustration or collage) depicting these ideas?
- What narrative will you integrate in the borders of your image?

Tar Beach Unit References

Art History Kids. n.d. "Faith Ringgold Books for Kids—Connecting Art to African American History." Accessed August 20, 2021. www.arthistorykids.com/blog/230.

The Art Story. n.d. "Faith Ringgold." Accessed August 20, 2021. www.theartstory.org/artist/ringgold-faith.

Hemmings, Jessica. 2020. "That's Not Your Story: Faith Ringgold Publishing on Cloth." *Parse* 11. parsejournal.com/article/thats-not-your-story-faith-ringgold-publishing-on-cloth.

MOMA. 2020. "Story Time: *Tar Beach* by Faith Ringgold." www.moma.org/magazine/articles/350

Norman Rockwell Museum. n.d. "Yuko Shimizu." Accessed August 20, 2021. unity.nrm.org/yuko-shimizu.

NPR. 2016. "Faith Ringgold Reads Her 1991 Children's Book *Tar Beach*." www.youtube.com/watch?v=h9RKJleFdBU

Spector, Nancy. n.d. "Faith Ringgold: *Woman on a Bridge* #1 of 5: Tar Beach." Collection online, Guggenheim. Accessed August 20, 2021. www.guggenheim.org/artwork/3719.

Tar Beach Unit Planning Chart

This evidence chart is a sample that focuses on the first part of the unit, during which students are reviewing Faith Ringgold's work.

Evidence Chart

Standards (Clear Learning Targets)	Specific Evidence of Learning Targets (Assessment Criteria)	Collection Strategies (Performance Tasks)
Visual Art Standard Art History and Cultural Context The student will describe how works of art are influenced by social, political, and economic factors.	■ Demonstration of close observation and analysis of an illustration using the elements of visual art (line, shape, color, form, texture, value, space) ■ Identification of how composition influences meaning using the principles of design (balance, movement, repetition/pattern, proportion, emphasis, contrast, unity, variety) ■ Identification of one's own interpretation of the work in relation to Ringgold's activism using art to bring forward lived experience of her community ■ Identification of social, political, and economic factors that influenced Ringgold's work, such as racism and prejudice	Brainstormed lists of ideas (formative assessment) Observations of elements, connections, memories, sensory connections Devised theater piece (summative assessment) Discussion (formative and summative assessment) ■ How does the artist use elements of design to tell a story? ■ How does the artist use the principles of design? ■ What do you see in the image that shows how Ringgold was pushing on the "social narratives" of the time?

Standards (Clear Learning Targets)	Specific Evidence of Learning Targets (Assessment Criteria)	Collection Strategies (Performance Tasks)
VUS.1 The student will demonstrate skills for historical thinking, zgeographical analysis, economic decision making, and responsible citizenship by synthesizing evidence from artifacts and primary and secondary sources to obtain information about events in Virginia and United States history.	<ul><li>Identification of themes in a primary source (as published imagery of the time)</li><li>Identification of choices made by the artist that reflect historical context, such as the positive depiction of African American life to counter balance stereotypes and the portrayal of strong and heroic Black women</li><li>Identification of themes and messages suggested by the art, such as the power of imagination</li><li>Identification of the use of symbolism (the use of art to represent an idea) in *Tar Beach*, such as the flight of Cassie as a depiction of imagination and transcending boundaries</li></ul>	Brainstormed lists of ideas (formative assessment) Devised theater piece (summative assessment) Discussion (formative and summative assessment) <ul><li>How does the story told by the Tar Beach image present a different perspective during the Civil Rights movement?</li><li>How might this artist's story quilt promote activism?</li></ul>

Unit Planning Chart

Standards	Specific Evidence of Learning Targets (Assessment Criteria)	Collection Strategies (Formative Assessment and Summative Tasks)

Recommended Resources

Storytelling Resources

Center for Digital Storytelling. www.storycenter.org.

Chase, Richard. 1976. "Soap, Soap, Soap." *In Grandfather Tales*, 115–122. New York: Houghton Mifflin Company.

Digital Storytelling. 2021. "The Educational Uses of Digital Storytelling." University of Houston Education. digitalstorytelling.coe.uh.edu/index.cfm.

Galdone, Paul. 1975. *The Gingerbread Boy*. New York: Houghton Mifflin Company.

Jacobs, Joseph, ed. 2007. "Lazy Jack." In *English Fairy Tales*. New York: Everyman's Library.

Lesson Planet. 2021. "Digital Storytelling Lesson Plans." www.lessonplanet.com/search?keywords=digital+storytelling&media=lesson. This site provides teachers with many examples of digital storytelling for a wide range of grade levels (e.g., the history of the American flag, grades 3–5; digital color poetry, grades 3–5; culture creation vs. culture consumption, grade 9; integrating grammar and literature, grades 9–12).

MacDonald, Margaret Read. 1986a. "Hic Hic Hic." In *Twenty Tellable Tales*. Chicago: American Library Association.

———. 1986b. "Jack and the Robbers." In *Twenty Tellable Tales*. Chicago: American Library Association.

———. 2000a. "Little Boy Frog and Little Boy Snake." In *Shake-It-Up Tales!*, 134–139. Little Rock, AR: August House.

———. 2000b. "What a Wonderful Life!" In *Shake-It-Up Tales!*, 115–124. Little Rock, AR: August House .

———. 2001a. "The Lost Mitten." In *The Parent's Guide to Storytelling*, 26–33. Little Rock, AR: August House.

———. 2001b. "The Wide Mouth Frog." In *The Parent's Guide to Storytelling*, 83–87. Little Rock, AR: August House.

———. 2006. *The Squeaky Door*. New York: HarperCollins Children's Books.

Morgan, Pierr. 1990. *The Turnip*. New York: Philomel.

National Storytelling Network. storynet.org/.

Paye, Won-Ldy, and Margaret H. Lippert. 2002. *Head, Body, Legs*. New York: Henry Holt and Company.

Pellowski, Anne. 1984a. "The Black Cat." In *The Story Vine*. New York: Aladdin.

———. 1984b. *The Story Vine: A Book of Unusual and Easy-to-tell Stories From Around the World*. New York: Macmillan.

———. 1987. "Brothers Tall and Brothers Small." In *The Family Storytelling Handbook*. New York: Simon & Schuster Children's Publishing.

———. 1995. "The King's Diamond Cross." In *The Storytelling Handbook*. New York: Simon & Schuster Children's Publishing.

Schimmel, Nancy. 1992a. "The Rain Hat." In *Just Enough to Make a Story*, 22–24. Berkeley, CA: Sisters' Choice Books and Recordings.

———. 1992b. "The Tailor." In *Just Enough to Make a Story*, 2–3. Berkeley, CA: Sisters' Choice Books and Recordings.

Story Center. 2021. "What We Do." www.storycenter.org/about.

University of Minnesota. 2021. "Digital Storytelling." digitalstory.umn.edu/.

Poetry Resources

Academy of American Poets. www.poets.org.

Bogard, Jenn. 2020. *The ABCs of Plum Island, Massachusetts: A Sampling of the Past and Present*. Portsmouth: Piscataqua Press.

Bogard, Jennifer M. and Mary C. McMackin. 2015. *Writing is Magic, or Is It? Using Mentor Texts to Develop the Writer's Craft*. Huntington Beach, CA: Shell Education.

Creech, Sharon. 2008. *Hate that Cat*. New York: HarperCollins Children's Books.

Dickinson, Emily. 1990. "Not in Vain." In *Emily Dickinson: Selected Poems*, 42, edited by Stanley Appelbaum. Mineola, NY: Dover Thrift Editions.

Franco, Betsy. 2009. *Messing Around the Monkey Bars*. Somerville, MA: Candlewick.

Heaney, Seamus. 1995. "Scaffolding." In *Death of a Naturalist*. London: Faber and Faber.

———. 1999. "The Rain Stick." In *Opened Ground: Selected Poems 1966–1996*. London: Faber and Faber.

Hughes, Langston. (1932) 2007. "Dreams." In *The Dream Keeper and Other Poems*. New York: Knopf Books for Young Readers.

Katz, Alan. 2008. *Oops!* New York: Simon & Schuster Children's Publishing.

Kipling, Rudyard. 2007. "If–." In *Kipling: Poems*, 170–171. New York: Everyman's Library.

Nesbitt, Kenn. 2006. "The Aliens Have Landed." In *The Aliens Have Landed at Our School*. Minnetonka, MN: Meadowbrook Press.

The Poem Farm. www.poemfarm.amylv.com.

Poetry Foundation. www.poetryfoundation.org.

Prelutsky, Jack. 1984. *New Kid on the Block*. New York: Greenwillow Books.

———. 1996. *A Pizza the Size of the Sun*. New York: Greenwillow Books.

———. 2005. *Raining Pigs and Noodles*. New York: HarperCollins.

———. 2008. "Be Glad Your Nose Is on Your Face " In *Be Glad Your Nose Is on Your Face and Other Poems: Some of the Best of Jack Prelutsky*, 152. New York: Greenwillow Books.

Shields, Carol D. 2003. *Almost Late to School*. New York: Dutton Children's Books.

Silverstein, Shel. 1974. *Where the Sidewalk Ends*. New York: HarperCollins.

———. 1981. *A Light in the Attic*. New York: HarperCollins.

———. 1996. *Falling Up*. New York: HarperCollins.

Soto, Gary. 1995. "Oranges." In *Gary Soto: New and Selected Poems*, 72–73. San Francisco: Chronicle Books.

Viorst, Judith. 1982. "If I Were in Charge of the World." In *If I Were in Charge of the World and Other Worries*, 2. New York: Simon & Schuster.

Music Resources

Decolonizing the Music Room. 2021. "Our Mission." decolonizingthemusicroom.com/mission. This website helps teachers develop critical practices through research, training, and discourse to build a more equitable future and includes songs/stories, resources, and videos.

Dunyo, Kwasi, and Karen Howard. 2020. *Dance Like a Butterfly: Songs from Liberia, Senegal, Nigeria, and Ghana*. Chicago: Gia Publications.

Folkstreams. 2020. "A National Preserve of American Folklore Films." www.folkstreams.net/about.php. This nonprofit is dedicated to finding, preserving, contextualizing, and showcasing documentary films on American traditional culture.

Global Music Project. www.globalmusicproject.org.

Jones, Bessie. 1972. *Step It Down: Games, Plays, Songs and Stories From the Afro-American Heritage*. Athens: The University of Georgia Press.

Library of Congress. www.loc.gov. Audio and video recordings of music and interviews.

Litz, Ron. 2020. "How to Use Art to Teach History." www.edutopia.org/article/how-use-art-teach-history.

Pascale, Louise. 2011. *Qu Qu Qu Barg-e-Chinaar: Children's Songs from Afghanistan*. Cambridge, MA: Children's Songs from Afghanistan. www.afghansongbook.org/.

Peterson, Elizabeth. 2018. "Teach SEAL (Social Emotional Artistic Learning) While Listening to Music." *The Inspired Classroom*. theinspiredclassroom.com/2018/01/teach-sel-listening-music.

Putumayo World Music. 2021. "Putumayo Kids Corner." www.putumayo.com/kids-corner.

Smithsonian Folkways Recordings. 2021. "Explore." Smithsonian Institution. folkways.si.edu. This website offers audio recordings and world music curricular resources and lessons from the Smithsonian Folkways network.

Sound Resources

Schafer, R. Murray. 1992. *A Sound Education: 100 Exercises in Listening and Sound-making*. Indian River, Ontario, Canada: Arcana Editions.

Instrument-Making Resources

deBeer, Sara, ed. 1995 *Open Ears: Musical Adventures for a New Generation*. Roslyn, NY: Ellipsis Kids.

Langstaff, John, and Ann Sayre Wiseman. 2003. *Making Music: 70 Improvisational Musical Instruments to Make and Play*. North Adams, MA: Storey Publishing.

Sabbeth, Alex. 1997. *Rubber-Band Banjos and a Java Jive Bass: Projects and Activities on the Science of Music and Sound.* New York: John Wiley and Songs.

Videos

Alarik, Scott. "Bessie Jones." Video, 7:43. 2015. Video about the life of Bessie Jones. scottalarik.com/index.php?page=video&category=Folk_Films_by_Scott_Alarik&display=362&from=0.

Honda. 2007a. "Great Car Commercial Honda." www.youtube.com/watch?v=DIaK8q5HT7k.

———. 2007b. "Honda Civic Choir: Rehearsal." www.youtube.com/watch?v=hyayFJ5Qzjs.

McFerrin, Bobby. 2009. "Bobby McFerrin and the Power of the Pentatonic Scale " www.ted.com/talks/bobby_mcferrin_hacks_your_brain_with_music.html. In this fun, three-minute performance from the World Science Festival, musician Bobby McFerrin uses the pentatonic scale to reveal one surprising result of the way our brains are wired.

National Film Board of Canada. 2017. "R. Murray Schafer: Listen." www.youtube.com/watch?v=rOlxuXHWfHw.

Pascale, Louise. 2015. "Returning Music to the Children of Afghanistan " www.youtube.com/watch?v=t1UWvPJ5WcU.

Perpetuum Jazzile. 2009. "Choir (Perpetuum Jazzile) Create a Rainstorm with Hands." www.youtube.com/watch?v=BC8re5HvOGI. This is a great performance by Perpetuum Jazzile using only their hands to create a sound story. You can almost smell the rain!

Stomp Out Loud. 2011. "Stomp!" www.youtube.com/watch?v=fN5T8y8bCJ4. Rhythm and garbage can make sense. This video includes 45 minutes of footage from the fantastic group Stomp.

Zander, Benjamin. 2008. "The Transformative Power of Classical Music." www.ted.com/talks/benjamin_zander_on_music_and_passion.html. Benjamin Zander has two infectious passions: classical music and helping all of us realize our untapped love for it—and by extension our untapped love for all new possibilities, new experiences, and new connections.

Creative Movement Resources

Creative Dance Center. 2020. "BrainDance Adaptations & Variations." creativedance.org/about/braindance.

Breakthroughs International. 2018. "The Brain Gym® Program." www.braingym.org.

Jacob's Pillow Archives: Dance Interactive and Online Database. www.jacobspillow.org/archives.

Visual Art Resource

Google Arts and Culture. artsandculture.google.com.

Drama Resource

Drama-Based Instruction: Activating Learning Through the Arts. dbp.theatredance.utexas.edu/.

General Arts Integration Resources

ArtsEdge at the Kennedy Center. artsedge.kennedy-center.org/artsedge.html.

Berkshire Regional Arts Integration Network. Brainworks.mcla.edu.

Diaz, Gene and Martha Berry McKenna, eds. 2017. *Preparing Educators for Arts Integration: Placing Creativity at the Center of Learning.* New York, NY: Teachers College Press.

Institute for Arts Integration and Steam. artsintegration.com/.

Research Resource

The Arts Education Partnership. 2021. "ArtsEdSearch." www.artsedsearch.org/. "ArtsEdSearch, a project of the Arts Education Partnership, is an online clearinghouse of research focused on the outcomes of arts education for students and educators, both during and outside the school day."